Raw Living

■ Detox your life and eat the high energy way

Kate Wood

Grub Street ■ London

To Chris, Reuben, Ethan, Zachary, Alxxx, Shazzie, Evie and Dani, for loving me enough to let me have my cake and eat it.

Published by Grub Street
4 Rainham Close, London SW11 6SS
email: food@grubstreet.co.uk
web: www.grubstreet.co.uk

Text Copyright © Kate Wood 2007
Copyright this edition © Grub Street 2007
Design by Lizzie Ballantyne

The moral right of the author has been asserted

A CIP catalogue record for this book is available from the British Library

ISBN 978-1-904943-74-7

Printed and bound by MPG, Bodmin, Cornwall

Grub Street Publishing only uses FSC (Forest Stewardship Council) paper for its books.

■ Contents

■ Foreword

When Kate Wood's first book, *Eat Smart, Eat Raw*, came out, I was so excited! Having read a dozen or so raw books from the USA, here was the UK's first raw recipe book to include ingredients that I know, love and can find in the shops!

Kate's book was so practical, I actually used the recipes. What a revelation for me! Now, after seeing the recipes in her second book, I am so glad that Kate has done it again.

I have a confession to make. Over the past year, I've been eating Kate's food at every opportunity. OK, I have a further confession to make, I haven't been making her recipes, she has. I've been loitering in her large sofa'd up kitchen and marvelling at the way she just presents me with a bowl, a smile and a question such as, 'Would you like some spinach cakes?' I enjoy the spinach cakes, I enjoy the company, and then I'm presented with a delicious pudding and the same smile as before. Her eldest son Reuben does the same, 'I've made some sweetcorn and almond soup. Would you like some?' Then he gently warms it and hands me a bowl, topped with crunchy bits. My daughter Evie wanders over to the dehydrator, which is always on, always making something. 'I want a biscuit!' She demands. Kate produces tomato crisps, biscuits and flapjacks for Evie to enjoy.

This is the essence of *Raw Living*. It's not just a collection of raw ingredients thrown together haphazardly. It's a raw family's gift destined to help us all create wonderful food choices for our families.

Raw Living is for everyone. We all know we need more fruit, vegetables and raw foods in our diet. So many more of us are now listening to the cues that our bodies are giving us: 'Be gentle with me, nourish me, love me, give me fresh air, snuggles and love, and I'll give you the best life ever.' We're all waking up to the fact that lighter living in all ways is the only way that makes sense. No nutritionist ever said, 'Eat more burgers and chips!' *Raw Living* offers us so many ways in which to nourish ourselves, that our bodies can cross it off its list of things to remind us to do.

Kate is the mother of three raw home-schooled boys. She's an author of two books. She's a company director, she has a shop and a cafe. She also likes to party! She manages to do all this because the foods she eats gives her the energy to do it. *Raw Living* is an infinite energy bank. Kate is a true example of a superbeing, and you can be too, just by eating her food. OK, you may not get to hang out in her kitchen, but you can eat *Raw Living*'s recipes - it's surely the next best thing!

Kate is also one of the leading lights in the Raw Chocolate Revolution. She's created more delicious chocolates, cakes, biscuits and savouries than anyone else I know. Some of them are in this book, so if you can't reach her shop, you can still experience them. Aren't you lucky?

So without further ado, all that remains to be said is: 'Let them eat, Kate!'

Shazzie
Author and managing director of Rawcreation Ltd

■ Introduction

Healthy eating is officially 'here'. It seems you can't move these days for nutritionists advising you what to eat, celebrities endorsing a new diet regime, governments issuing strategies, or the media supplying alarming statistics. We are becoming a nation of people who take our health seriously, who want to eat the right things, who want to be slim, fit and youthful. We are realising that in some foods quality has deteriorated over the past fifty years, to the point where we can no longer get all the nutrients we need from it. And there are so many more stresses to contend with, which deplete our reserves: environmentally in the form of pollution, chemicals in the home, and electromagnetic radiation; and socially, in the fast-paced, high pressured lives so many of us live these days. If we do not look after ourselves properly, inevitably we become prey to one of the numerous symptoms of ill-health that affect us all; from general fatigue and muddle-headedness, through to asthma, eczema and psoriasis, all the way to cancer, heart disease and diabetes.

But it can be very hard to bridge that gap between our good intentions and our day-to-day realities. You may have read half a dozen times now that you need to get lots of Essential Fatty Acids (EFAs) to help prevent depression, but you're still not really sure what to do with that bottle of flax oil at the back of your fridge. You've realised your children's diet is low in minerals, but how do you get them to eat their greens? You're ready to kick the Dairy Milk habit, but what are you going to replace it with? Or you may simply not have the time and energy to research thoroughly the new foods you should be eating to achieve vitality. That's where *Raw Living* steps in.

If you examine all the various nutritional theories and diet plans closely, all that advice has a lot in common. Jill says add a little ingredient X, Paul wants you to add supplement Y, and for Caroline, cutting out Z is the key. But break it down and they are all saying the same things:

- ■ Eat more fruit and vegetables
- ■ Drink more water
- ■ Eat more healthy fats
- ■ Take some extra vitamin and mineral supplements

This is *Raw Living* in a nutshell. The basis of a raw food diet is raw fruit and vegetables, preferably organically and locally grown, and eaten seasonally. To that add liquids in the form of pure water and fresh juices; fats such as nuts, seeds, avocados and olives; sprouted grains and pulses; and superfoods like bee pollen and spirulina (a microalgae). You need to avoid meat, dairy, gluten, sugar, and all processed foods, but one of the joys of the raw food diet is that it is effective if you follow it at least 50 % of the time. So you could have a raw breakfast, a cooked lunch, and a salad and something cooked for tea, or eat raw all day and then have a cooked dinner. Chances are if you picked up this book, you are doing some of that already. See? Eating raw is easy, because it's intuitively what we want to do. You don't have to give up your favourite foods, but you will find over time that if you stick with it, your taste buds will change, and you will stop craving junk food and start craving superfood!

I don't want to tell you what to do; there are enough experts around to do that. What I do want to do is to open the door to a whole new world of raw food cuisine. Raw foods are a revelation. After well over a decade of eating raw, I am more excited about this food than ever. I am still constantly discovering new ingredients or coming across new combinations. If I eat out at a raw friend's house, I am invariably delighted by the variety and individuality of their cuisine. Raw foods inspire us to fulfil our creative potential, both in the kitchen and out of it! Eating this way is a real pleasure: simple and easy to prepare, this food can be savoured and enjoyed however busy your day, and fuel you with energy to cope with life's demands. When you eat foods that are fresh, locally, seasonally and organically grown, you are tapping into the infinite life force of the earth, you are accessing divine energy, and it tastes good.

This collection of recipes consists of all the dishes that my family has particularly loved over the last few years. At the time I was creating them, I had three sons under the age of seven and little time or energy to spend slaving in the kitchen. I had to make sure the food was ready quickly; but I also had to make sure it was going to be eaten, and not left on the plate. So here they are; a unique collection of raw food recipes that will taste amazing, make you feel amazing, and still leave you with time to get out of the kitchen and on with your life.

I really loved writing this book. Going back to the information made me realise all over again how exciting raw foods are. It is such an easy concept to take on board, and its effects are nothing short of revolutionary. I have been travelling on this path for many years now but it's human nature to take things for granted and forget how far we have come. These days I am in the blessed position where most of my friends and the people I surround myself with are rawfooders; it's not even something I think about anymore. Putting the information together for this book has helped me see it with fresh eyes. I am passionate about the implications of the raw food diet for our society. When everyone starts to honestly take responsibility for their own health, to take their lives back into their own hands and empower themselves with the true facts about human potentiality and vitality, what kind of a world will we be creating then? When everyone wakes up feeling as super-charged and enthusiastic about life as the average rawfooder, what amazing realities will we be able to manifest? One of my most dearly held maxims is to 'be the change you wish to see in the world.' This is my main motivating force for eating a raw food diet, and why I feel it is so important. Eating raw provides us with one of the most integral tools for living a life of joy and abundance, for being a positive inspiration to those around us, and to counteracting all the negative and awful things that happen in the world day after day.
I believe the best way to make the world a better place is to be a force for good in every way you can, at every moment possible; I believe complaining, fighting and protesting just contributes more unhappiness to the overall global situation. After twenty years of thinking this way, I can see sure signs that humanity is beginning to learn that there is a bigger picture, and I am often overwhelmed by the massive shifts that could be made once this consensus becomes reality. Now we are at a time where this is truly possible, and by holding this book in your hands and accessing the information I have built up after years of study and experience, you have found a wonderful key for really making your life a shining example. How fantastic is that?

Kate Wood

■ Conception and pregnancy

Conception is the start of an amazing journey into parenthood, and the more you can do to prepare yourself and build a solid foundation, the easier it will be to springboard into the chaos children bring into your lives. If you are at your optimum physically, it will enable you to conceive quickly, carry the baby successfully, give your child a great start in life, and build up your stores for the intensely depleting work of pregnancy and breastfeeding. For at least three months before starting to try for a baby, if circumstances allow, it is wise to examine your diet, your emotional well-being, and embark on a cleansing and detoxification programme.

Like many young people, before I had children, I rarely got ill, had little stress in my life and few real responsibilities. I ate sensibly, but didn't give much thought to where I got my calcium or iron from. I didn't have a GP. I don't remember even suffering from the occasional cold. So not only did the prospect of parenthood make me think seriously about how I was going to care for a child without following the conventional models, it made me reassess my own health provision. Carrying a baby puts untold stress on the body, and it doesn't stop at birth; breastfeeding demands huge amounts of physical resources too. Each time you have a child your body is left weakened and depleted, and unless you take a proactive approach to your health, each subsequent baby is likely to bring health complications as the stress of parenthood takes its toll.

In the UK, on average, it takes a couple seven months to conceive. If you are fortunate enough to be in the position of actively trying for a baby, there are many simple dietary measures you can take to increase your fertility and ease the transition into motherhood. This isn't a time to be embarking on a radical healthy eating plan, but there are a few easy and gentle changes you can make. If you are too extreme, you will only yo-yo back to your old ways when you get pregnant, which puts stress on your body. If you go on a detoxing programme when you are pregnant and breastfeeding, the baby can absorb the toxins that your body is getting rid of, through the placenta or in your milk, so it is wise to avoid cleansing at this time. Many women find it hard to keep up healthy eating habits when pregnant, particularly in the first trimester, so best to eat your greens now, before they make you throw up!

One of the most basic ways you can increase your fertility is to cut out alcohol, tobacco, and caffeine. In his book *Optimum Nutrition Before, During and After Pregnancy*, Patrick Holford cites research showing that drinking just one cup of coffee a day can half your chances of conceiving, as can drinking alcohol daily, that smoking damages the quality of your eggs, and reduces the number capable of producing a baby and a diet high in antioxidants has been shown to aid fertility, especially in women over 35, so eating lots of raw fruit and veg is a must. Being both underweight and overweight can lessen your chances of conceiving. In one study, nearly three quarters of women with unexplained infertility conceived naturally once they stopped dieting and achieved their optimal weight. Conversely, if you are overweight, this can disturb your hormone balance and stop you ovulating. Losing just 10% of weight can dramatically stimulate ovulation.

The two essential minerals for fertility are selenium and zinc. Less than one in ten people in the UK receive their Recommended Daily Allowance (RDA) for zinc; good sources are pumpkin seeds, chick peas, cheese, and tahini. The best source of dietary selenium is Brazil nuts, which contain 839 mcg in 30 g/1 oz nuts (the RDA is 55 mcg!). Another good source is whole grains, such as wheat. However, due to intensive agriculture over the last century, and the extensive use of chemicals and pesticides on the land, the UK soil is generally depleted, and doesn't contain the levels of minerals it used to, selenium being one of those minerals. On the vitamin front, B6 is the one to watch out for, found in cauliflower, watercress, bananas and broccoli. Also important is a daily dose of EFAs, which you can find in flax seed and hemp oil. If you don't currently take any superfoods, now is a really good time to start, for your baby's sake. Good ones for fertility are bee pollen (which is high in B6 and zinc), and maca (*Lepidium Meyenii*), also known as nature's Viagra (see Superfoods chapter).

Nausea in pregnancy is a result of the huge surge of hormones that pervade the body at this time. But in some primitive tribal cultures, morning sickness is unknown. I believe the degree to which you get sick is partially connected to how many toxins you have stored in your body, as well as emotional and lifestyle factors. Also affecting you is how much stress you are under during the pregnancy; stress creates toxicity in the system. You can help yourself by doing a liver cleanse before you try and conceive. Every morning for six weeks, first thing in the morning, take a tablespoon of olive oil mixed with a tablespoon of fresh lemon juice. It may not taste good to you and could well make you nauseous in itself, but it will help clear out congestion in the liver, and that should put you in good stead for what is to come. Wheatgrass is also an excellent liver cleanser. It is easy and cheap to grow your own, or you can buy ready-made trays from health food stores or online. Drinking 4 tablespoons of wheatgrass every morning is one of the best ways of detoxifying I have come across, because of its high chlorophyll content. Chlorophyll is similar in composition to human blood, and oxygenates the cells. It is also fantastic for balancing blood sugar, and low blood sugar can be another cause of nausea.

It's vital to stay hydrated, especially if you are vomiting regularly. Many women find it next to impossible to drink pure water at the beginning. If you can't face it, try herbal teas, or some very diluted fruit concentrate; some women find carbonated water palatable when plain water is not. Ideally you should be aiming for at least two litres of liquid a day, if not three. Ginger and lemon are popular home remedies. Make some tea with grated ginger root, a slice of organic unwaxed lemon and hot water, or if you have a juicer, add a piece of ginger (as much as you can stomach) and a slice of lemon and juice with apples and/or pears.

Once you've conceived, you're into a whole new unexplored territory foodwise. It's unfair, but at the time when eating healthily is probably more important than it has ever been in your life, it becomes very hard to control your desires for what you do and don't want to eat. I knew I was pregnant the second time because I developed a strong craving for Marmite on toast, neither foods which I usually eat, and the exact same craving I had had with my first pregnancy. I'm sure it's no coincidence that Marmite contains beneficial vitamins and minerals for the developing foetus, and many women report it alleviates sickness. My body knew it wanted B vitamins, and knew where it had got them in the past, so sent me in that direction. Many women find they want very bland and simple foods, without rich sauces, and however healthy you are, you are likely to find yourself craving rubbishy foods – anything that's comforting and calming. It's important to strike a balance and look after yourself in all areas of your life as much as you can; this is likely to be your last chance to get leisure time for a few years! Don't be hard on yourself for wanting unhealthy foods and don't deny yourself what you want to make you happy; but balance the junk with some nutrient dense foods that you still find palatable. The key to optimum health in this period is through finding a few really nutritious foods that you love and making sure you get them down you as much as possible. You won't have much room in your stomach for big meals, but you need to maintain your strength up, so keep the focus on juices and superfoods. Eating raw is really not the priority: making sure you are sending your body all the love you can and feeding it vitamins and minerals any way you can is where your attention should go. Trying to be too controlling over your diet at this time is unhelpful and dangerous. If you haven't done the work on your health prior to conception, now is really not the time to be pushing yourself. Love yourself for exactly who you are, and revel in this unique and fascinating period in your life.

■ Breastfeeding

Breastfeeding can be a wonderfully bonding experience for mother and baby, and it is truly amazing to watch your little one flourish on the miracle fluid your body makes. But it is really hard work! Whereas pregnancy demands only 300 extra calories a day from the body, breastfeeding demands about 500. And whereas pregnancy is a time to (hopefully) rest, nurture yourself, and bathe in the near universal good wishes of everyone around you, the commitment of breastfeeding is given little to no recognition in our society. You are literally, giving of yourself, usually for endless hours, day and night, while you are expected to competently carry on with all your other responsibilities too. No wonder most women give up before the first year is out. But there is no doubt that the longer you breastfeed for, the better start your child has in life. In my experience, most children who are allowed to self-wean do so around 36 months old, although many go on longer.

So having just gone through the miracle of pregnancy and childbirth, when your body has really been put through its paces, it has to deal with this most demanding of tasks, maybe for several years. Most women find themselves ravenously hungry in the first few months after the birth. It is vital, for your health and that of the baby, that you take really good care of yourself. You might not get time to nurture yourself with long baths, uninterrupted time with your partner, or Sunday lie-ins, but you can eat well. In fact, it may be a welcome opportunity for you to eat as much as you like without having to worry about putting on weight!

Between the three boys, I breastfed continuously for nearly ten years, and was on a high raw diet throughout this time. I searched long and hard for the answers to good health that would help sustain me, and not leave me feeling exhausted and depleted. Raw foods have without a doubt been a major factor in allowing me to give my all to my children, and still have some energy left for myself. But they have their limits. Breastfeeding is so demanding on the body that you need to consume huge quantities of nutrients, and however carefully you eat, you're not going to be able to get enough from your food. Overeating is never good, puts a strain on your digestive system, and makes you tired and sluggish. In my opinion, the answers lie in superfoods and juices, which when used correctly, give you sustained energy, without creating additional work for the body.

You need to ensure you're getting your protein, to help build baby's body up. Lots of sprouts are essential: lentil, chick pea, and mung bean are wonderful. Too many nuts and seeds can be mucus-forming: if you overeat on them, particularly if they are not soaked first, you may find your child starts producing lovely thick green or yellow snot. The best ones to have are hemp, sesame, pumpkin and sunflower, making sure they are soaked for at least a few hours. I always try to soak them overnight, and then leave them to sprout for a whole day if possible. Sesame is a powerhouse of nutrients: particularly needed for breastfeeding are calcium, iron, zinc, and the B vitamins, especially B6. Zinc is really important – according to leading UK nutritionist Patrick Holford, only one in twenty people in the UK gets the recommended daily amount of zinc in the diet. Good sources are pumpkin seeds, chick peas, and tahini. B6 can be found in cauliflower, watercress, bananas and broccoli (one banana provides over 50% of the RDA), and don't forget the B12 – the only way to be 100% sure with that one is to take it in supplement form. As for calcium, breastfeeding women need a whopping 550 mg extra per day - look for it in green veg (particularly broccoli), seaweeds, sesame seeds and maca.

You also need a good supply of fats to make lovely rich breast milk. Again, don't overdo the nuts and seeds, but do include raw oils such as olive and flax, as well as avocados and olives. Flax oil is always important in the diet, but never more so than at this stage: try to include 1-2 tablespoons a day. If you're not strictly raw you may want to include some molasses in your diet: rich in iron and calcium, it's very good mixed with tahini and spread on crackers and Essene bread. Nutritional yeast flakes are not a raw product either, but chock full of B vitamins, and make a tasty addition to most dinners.

Some days, I used to feel very much like a cow: I did little but eat my greens and produce milk, going back and forth between baby and kitchen from morning to night, alternately grazing and being milked. My green juice is my wonder drink, my lifesaver, the tonic I absolutely could not do without. Never, since my discovery of raw foods, have I experienced such a profound shift in health as I did when I started on green juice every day. It took my diet onto a whole new level, partly because it is an excellent way of getting nutrients into the body, particularly the minerals which are so essential for breastfeeding. But equally beneficial are the deep cleansing and alkalising properties of the juice that flood my system, keep me in balance, and help me to make better food choices throughout the day. I drink at least half a litre or one pint a day, usually a combination of broccoli, fennel (which is good for milk production), celery, cucumber, and parsley (for iron). You can't beat some locally grown, in season greens such as spring greens, chard, or kale, or if you like your wild foods, dandelion and nettle are wonderful leaves to juice. I could not get enough broccoli: in one form or another, I had about a kilo a day. It's one of the most nutritious vegetables, and exceptionally high in calcium and the B vitamins.

Remember, you are effectively providing your baby with its first food, and if your diet is lacking, so is theirs. To ensure the good health of your baby, it is vital that you over compensate, packing as much nutrition in you as possible, rather than risk leaving your child deficient. For this reason, superfoods are really the only way to go. Superfoods are natural plant foods that are incredibly dense nutritionally, and are much more easily assimilated by the body than artificially produced supplements. There is a huge variety to choose from these days, but the ones I recommend for breastfeeding are bee pollen and maca. Bee pollen has a delicious sweet taste, and gives you an instant energy hit, so you can have some whenever you start to flag. It's a complete food, containing all the vitamins and minerals essential to the body, but particularly noteworthy for mums because of its high levels of vitamin B6 and zinc. Maca is great for balancing your hormones, and can help lift your mood and stave off hunger when you're sitting feeding all day. It is also used for stamina and endurance, as well as being a complete protein and high in many vitamins and minerals, including calcium and zinc.

I also recommend drinking plenty of water. You may be shocked at first at the amounts you need to drink, but think of all those hours you sit feeding, and how much fluid is leaving your body in the form of breast milk. I personally used to drink four litres a day: one in the morning, before breakfast, another before lunch, another in the afternoon, and one more before bed. It is very important to stay hydrated to ward off fatigue – I would say aim for at least three litres a day.

Breastfeeding is not discussed much because it's not something we will all do in our lives: even when you've discounted the male half of the population, many women don't have children, and many of those that do, choose not to, or can't, feed their babies themselves. But it is something that most of us experience, as newborns ourselves, and as such it is crucially important because it provides us with our physical foundation, as our little bodies build and grow. The nutrition that we receive in the womb and in the first few years at the breast can set us up for a lifetime of good health. It seems to me indisputable that all women who carry this great honour and responsibility should do the best they can to ensure the well-being of the next generation.

■ Children

Feeding children is a minefield, whether they're raw or not. When they're little, it's impossible to know what they want to eat, resulting in many wasted meals and frustrating feeding times. When they get older what they want isn't always what we would want for them! As raw foodists, it's made even harder by the lack of concrete information on suitable foods for children; there are so many differing opinions on what are the right foods for adults, and there has been virtually no research on how children's needs differ from ours. On the one hand, you might consider weaning your child on fruit, as it is easy to digest and easy to mash. But then you might worry about the amount of sugar in the diet, so consider veg instead. But raw veg are much harder to purée and not so tasty. Do you add in fats for sustenance, or are they too dense for children? What about sprouted grain crackers, do they make good finger foods, or are they too denatured for baby's sensitive palate? If you listened to all the 'experts' you would end up feeding them nothing, but that is the last thing you want to do; you want a big, healthy well-fed baby to demonstrate to all the concerned relatives and healthcare professionals how your offspring is thriving on your chosen diet and that you are a responsible parent.

I am sorry to say there is no simple answer. I wish I could say 'give them this, this, and this', and all us mums could rest peacefully in our beds at night. The thing is children are their own people, with their own characteristics, and their own likes and dislikes. When Reuben was born, I had all these fixed ideas on how I was going to wean him, a carefully programmed, well-balanced diet, gently introducing him to a wide range of healthy raw foods. But he was having none of it, steadfastly refusing whatever I put in front of him unless it was cooked. What I learnt is that children are our mirrors; whatever you eat while they are in the womb influences their taste buds, setting down their desires and cravings for their first few years. Reuben has a taste for cooked foods, because I ate them when I was pregnant and breastfeeding; Ethan doesn't, but he has a very sweet tooth, as I was eating a lot of fruit when I was carrying and feeding him. As parents we are their role models; if they see one or other of us eating cooked foods, you can be sure they will want some too. You can't set higher standards for your children than for yourself, it just doesn't work; if you have cooked foods in the house you are going to have to accept that they will be eating them too. So, like most things in life, it comes right back to where we are in ourselves. All we can do is to set the right example with what we eat, and sure as durian is durian, they will follow - eventually.

Don't spend your day in the kitchen trying to find something they relish, or you are creating issues around food. If you let them see that it is a big deal to you what they eat, they quickly catch on it is one of your 'buttons' that they can press to wind you up - you are setting yourself up for power struggles and miserable meal times. On the other hand, don't starve them on a diet of grapes and cucumber; children need sustenance, they need reserves, because they're growing so fast. If there are one or two foods that they will eat, that seem to suit them, like bananas or avocados, don't worry, just let them get on with it – in a month or two they'll be on to something else. If they refuse everything you prepare, just make extras of what you have. Most children go through fussy stages where it seems like they're not eating anything; but no child will willingly starve themselves (they will also go through stages where they want to eat you out of house and home!). If you keep pandering to them and making them special dishes, they are going to keep demanding their own meals and creating a whole load of work for you. It's a hard balancing act, to make sure they're eating enough without making an issue out of it, but the trick really is to just let them see you enjoying your food, and they will want some too.

The secret of feeding healthy children is all the little extras that you can add in without them noticing. There are a number of things you can include in their diet that they will barely taste, but will really boost their nutritional levels. The two most important ones are water and flax seed oil. I could write a whole chapter on the importance of getting enough of these, but suffice to say that they will make a huge difference to your child's mood, energy, and ability to learn and concentrate.

Few children drink enough water – every time mine are hungry, I tell them to have a cup of water first. So often we mistake the thirst signal for hunger. By the time they are five, you should be aiming for one litre a day, upping it to two by the time they are teenagers. Flax oil is the best vegan source of EFAs, the omega 6 and omega 3 oils. Most flax oils are processed in such a way to ensure that they are still raw. Children need at least a teaspoon a day, preferably a tablespoon. We can also find it in flax seeds and hemp seeds, but it is much harder for the body to absorb. If you can't get them to take flax oil, you can always massage them with it; they will absorb it through the skin. We have lecithin with our flax oil: it contains phosphatidyl-choline which helps with brain development, and it also aids in the emulsification of fats, enabling the body to absorb the EFAs better.

I am also a great believer in superfoods. Our soil is so depleted now that even if we eat organic food, the nutrient levels are still lower than they were just fifty years ago. Superfoods are particularly invaluable for fussy children, acting as a safety net, so you know at least they've had something decent on those days when they don't want to eat. Bee pollen and Klamath Lake blue-green algae are both natural food sources which contain everything the body needs to sustain life. Children only need tiny amounts, so it needn't be costly; about 1/2 teaspoon a day, or they will be too restless and unable to sleep.

Sea vegetables are the most mineral rich foods that there are, and there's a wide variety to choose from. We have kelp powder (just 1/2 teaspoon for the children), and Clearspring Atlantic sea salad (a blend of sea vegetables) or nori flakes on our lunch (alongside nutritional yeast flakes which aren't raw, but are a great source of B vitamins, and children seem to love the taste). For dinner, I often put arame (or 'worms'!) in their salad. They love nori sheets (kids think it's great fun to eat paper, I remember I loved rice paper as a child), and a fun meal is to make a couple of tasty pâtés, put them on the table with some sprouts, and let them make their own nori rolls. Dulse and wakame make great **seaweed crisps** (p 166) if you rinse them (wakame needs soaking for ten minutes) and put them in the dehydrator for about six hours, until crispy. While we're on the subject, tomato crisps (see *Eat Smart Eat Raw*) are another favourite in our family. We spread nut butter on them and sandwich two together.

For years, the boys' favourite was pasta – I cooked some rice or corn pasta and drowned it in **raw pasta sauce** (p 142). They're happy because they're getting pasta for dinner; I'm happy because they're getting tomatoes, celery, carrots, avocado... Thankfully, I've weaned them off the cooked dinners now, but I've used this trick a lot in the past: they think they're getting a cooked dinner, when you know they're getting their quota of raw as well. I used to make a soup by cooking potatoes and onions, then adding some raw veg and almond butter and blending it all up. You can do this with rice, millet, lentils: cook as normal, and when done add vegetables, seaweed, and nut butter, whatever you can sneak past them. The other thing that works great if they want cooked food is bartering. Make a deal with them – if you eat a carrot, you can have a rice cake; if you eat a banana you can have some yogurt. If they eat all their dinner, they can get a treat like a date or a sweetie in the bath. This system is fantastic because it gets you out of arguments; they don't have to do what you want, but if they don't, they won't get what they want – it's simple, and it worked for me.

Most children will prefer fruit over vegetables, so you've really got to encourage them to eat those green leafies and steer them away from too much sugar. Try not to let them eat more sweet fruit than veg, if you let them fill up on the sweet stuff you are encouraging a sugar habit and mood swings that you definitely don't want in a two year old or a teenager. It's far better that they eat lightly cooked vegetables than none at all. Things like kale and broccoli are fantastic just steamed or stir fried for a couple of minutes to soften them a little, and smothered in a creamy nut dresssing. Avoid too much dried fruit because of problems with tooth decay. One good way to start the day is with a smoothie, and bigger children may take pride and pleasure in making their own. They can invent their own recipes – a banana, some seasonal fruits, their favourite nut butter or flax oil, and a cup of water to blend. Banana ice cream is another favourite of ours – peel bananas, break into chunks, freeze for 12 hours, and process, preferably in a high power juicer, but a food processor or Vitamix will do. We had it for breakfast every day one summer - how fantastic is that, having ice cream for breakfast? When Ethan was going through one of his fussy stages, he had chocolate pudding with added flax oil and blue-green algae every day for lunch – and who can blame him, I had to stop myself from eating it all most days.

■ Children's parties

Christmas comes but once a year, birthdays however come once, twice, or maybe more, depending on the size of your family. At first, catering for a children's party can seem like every raw foodist's nightmare – the potential for conflicts over junk food is huge. In the early days I used to worry myself silly trying to prepare a feast that everyone would be happy with. Of course, you can't please all the people all the time, and despite my best efforts it never really worked. The main problem was that the more effort I put in, the more disappointed I was when people didn't appreciate, or even worse, didn't eat, my raw culinary creations. Or if I put 'healthy' cooked food out, like rice cakes or vegan cookies, I would be annoyed when that was all my children wanted to eat, while their cousins, accustomed to junk food, wouldn't touch them at all.

In my experience, children aren't really that interested in food at parties. They want to run around making a noise and a mess, and have far too much energy to actually sit still for any length of time and eat anything. You usually need far less than you think you are going to. For instance, at Ethan's last party I was doing dips and only had two carrots to go round five children and three adults. Whereas previously I would have sent Chris out on an emergency trip to the shops, I just did what I had, and what do you know, there was still some leftovers at the end.

The basic plan is to keep it simple. Don't try too hard to impress people with your gourmet raw cuisine, because no-one's going to be that bothered. As a general rule, don't put anything out that you don't mind your children eating a lot of. You can't argue about food in the middle of the party, and it would be mean to limit what they have – they need to feel that they can spoil themselves. So don't put out rice cakes unless you don't mind if that is all they end up eating. For older children, if they are absolutely adamant that they want crisps, veggie sausages, or whatever they had at a friend's party, then just buy enough so there's only a little bit to go round and they can't overdose on them. But if you can get away with it, it's better to leave that stuff out all together. You can bet that if you put out a big bowl of crisps and a big bowl of carrot sticks, all the crisps will get eaten and all the carrots will be left.

So just do the bare minimum. Dips are a basic that you can't go wrong with. Yellow, orange and red peppers, carrots, broccoli, and cucumber sticks for dipping are the most popular (celery always gets left). Do a couple of dips such as raw hummus, tomato ketchup (yes, really,

the recipe in *Eat Smart Eat Raw* makes a gorgeous dip), or tahini dip –
one vegetable based one and one nutty one for variety. Traffic light
biscuits are a winner. Arrange them on every child's plate before they
sit down, to start them off. Replace fatty, salty, fried potato chips with
tomato crisps. If you're catering for adults as well make a big green
salad and you should be covered.

Personally, I would steer away from desserts. A gathering of children
needs no encouragement in order to run around hyperactively.
Too much sugar and there are bound to be tears. All you need is a fruit
bowl so they can help themselves to grapes, apples, oranges or
bananas. If you're keen, you might want to make some sweeties
with nuts and dried fruit, or some dehydrated cookies. For Reuben's
birthday one year, he was insistent that we make raw cup cakes.
We made a cookie mix, some with oat groats and some with sprouted
wheat (you could use the flapjack recipe on p 215 and just add a little
extra water, 4 tablespoons would do, to make a cookie batter), and
spooned it into little paper cases. When they were dehydrated the next
day, we made a carob icing, and put a lexia raisin on the top for
decoration. Jelly and ice cream might also be worth a try, although not
for children used to dairy, sugar etc. who will probably find it too bland
and reject your efforts. Make the ice cream from frozen bananas, and
the jelly made from agar and juice or psyllium and puréed fruit.
It's messy (make sure they sit at the table to eat it), but delicious.

Another idea that children love is to make little fruit kebabs (p 182).
Buy a pack of cocktail sticks and assemble your chosen ingredients –
you want a selection of dried and fresh fruit. Skewer them as close to
eating time as possible, so they don't brown and become unappetizing.
Get your children to help you putting four or five items on the stick –
the possibilities are endless, but try and get a mix of fresh and dried
fruit on each. For some reason, children adore these little cocktail
sticks, and have as much fun making them as they will eating them.
If you don't mind the mess, you can make some carob sauce or cashew
cream to dip them into.

But best to save your energies for the birthday cake, which really is
your *pièce de resistance* and the one dish that everyone will remember.
If you are having lots of children who aren't used to raw foods, a fruit
tart is the most foolproof option. Make a crust with equal amounts of
dates and almonds, and fill it with whatever fruit is in season. In the
winter, you could slice apples and pears very thinly, and fill the crust

with those. In the summer, a selection of berries makes a wonderful option – blackberries, raspberries, blueberries and strawberries. Or you could try an exotic fruit combo such as mango and kiwi, two fruits that are always popular with children.

One more tip - always give tiny portions of cake. I find it very soul destroying to see all my wonderful food left over when all the children have taken a couple of mouthfuls and pushed it around the plate a bit. They can always come back for seconds, thirds, and even fourths! Psychologically, your children will feel a lot more indulged and spoiled if they have had three small portions of cake than one large one.

Finally, if you are inviting grannies and aunties to your party, who simply can't live without their cheese sandwiches, ask one special relative who enjoys catering if they could bring a big plate for everyone to share. Most people would prefer to do this than go hungry (or have to eat your rabbit food). If diplomacy is required, just explain that you will be doing lots of lovely food, but it's not the sort of thing that they usually eat, and would they like to bring a favourite dish (and maybe a few teabags) in case they want something else.

■ Sample Menu

Traffic light biscuits
Tomato crisps
Tahini dip
Tomato ketchup
Carrot, pepper and cucumber sticks
Leafy green salad
Birthday cake
Ice cream and jelly
Sweeties
Flapjacks
Fruit kebabs and carob sauce

■ Husbands (and other partners)

When I met my first husband, Chris, he was a vegetarian; over the course of five years he became 90% raw. When we were first together, he refused to have a salad for dinner because he claimed it wouldn't be substantial enough; I remember so clearly the day when I said I was planning to do baby new potatoes with our dinner, and he said, 'I'd prefer to have something raw'. So what happened along the way? Did I pester him, nag him, and badger him into going raw? Well, maybe a little. But everyone has to go on their own raw journey, and the beauty of raw foods is that they themselves are the best teachers.

Many women I speak to who come to raw foods after already having had a family, cite their husband's resistance to raw foods as one of the hardest obstacles to overcome. If you're uninformed, it's easy to dismiss it as another faddy diet, and see no reason to forsake all the favourite tastes to which you are accustomed. So women often try to carry on cooking for their men, but if you're anything like me, I find it impossible not to have a taste of something I'm making (just to check the flavours of course!). And if you're hungry and stressed and busy and tired, it's easy for that taste to turn into a few mouthfuls, or even dinner itself. So to make your life easier, if nothing else, you've got to show them that eating raw foods is something they want to do, as well as something they'll enjoy doing.

Men hate to be nagged. If they are going to eat raw, they must feel like it's their idea, they are doing it because they genuinely want to. Not only will most men dig their heels in and rebel if they think that you're (literally) trying to shove something down their throats, no-one's going to stick at it unless it's something they truly believe in. So leave some raw-food books lying around for him to read – Juliano's *Uncook Book* if you think he'll be tempted by all the yummy pictures, or try *Conscious Eating* by Gabriel Cousens if he's more likely to be persuaded by scientific facts. Ask if he'll come to a lecture by an inspirational speaker such as David Wolfe or Shazzie. If he really won't listen to you, ring up one of the many raw food practitioners around who offer consultations and they can assuage his doubts.

Make sure he has plenty of choice, and enough to fill him up, or he is going to reach for the cooked treats and fall back into old habits. Make raw versions of his cooked favourites. If you are able, invest in a dehydrator; transitioning a family from cooked to raw without one is hard. I have my dehydrator on for about three days a week, for biscuits, cakes, crackers, crisps, burgers, loaves etc. These raw treats, made from sprouted grains such as oats, buckwheat, wheat, rye and spelt, are a very satisfying alternative to conventional cakes and biscuits. When grains are milled into flour and cooked, the gluten in them makes them hard to digest, and plays havoc with blood sugar levels; sprouting releases enzymes which turn the starches into more easily digestible sugars, as well as increasing the nutritional content.

So hopefully by now, he's seen the sense in it, even if he still might not be keen to try it himself. In my experience, the best way to proceed is by compromise. For dinner every day, make one cooked dish, and one raw dish. Give yourself a large portion of raw (and a small portion of cooked if you want), and give him his usual cooked portion, with a small raw side dish. Make something really tasty, but only give him a little bit – leave him wanting more. Gradually, over the weeks and months, up the raw quotient, until one day you'll be able to leave out the cooked altogether.

Chris didn't need me to go on at him about the benefits of raw foods, because he started to feel them for himself. We are always talking about cooked foods being addictive – they are, for sure, the hardest addiction to fight. Recent research from the University of Wisconsin shows that junk food alters brain biochemistry with effects similar to drugs such as morphine, nicotine, or heroin! But you get hooked on raw foods too. When you have those days when you feel as light as a feather, your energy is soaring, and even when things go wrong you just know that it must have happened for a good reason; that feeling is addictive. We went to a party a few years back, and there was a lot of raw food, but also lots of vegan cake and ice cream. Chris ate loads of cake, but I didn't care – I knew he'd have a cooked food hangover the next day, and he'd know for himself that he didn't want a wife who baked! All you can do is trust that if you guide your husband gently on to the path, if he's got any sense at all, he'll be leaping along the way in no time, and maybe even overtake you.

And if you're a male raw fooder reading this book, and you're saying, 'What about me?' I say, 'Wow, isn't your lady lucky?' There's a lot of raw women around who can't find a man who is as into looking after their bodies as they are. If you're already in a relationship, your partner is very fortunate to be with such a switched on guy. And if you're single, you've got your pick of the raw goddesses to choose from.

■ Aphrodisiacs

The public image of the raw food diet is changing. A few years ago when I told people I ate a raw diet, the most common question would be, 'What do you eat?' And when I told people the sort of things we had for dinner - burgers, Thai, pasta, sushi, not to mention the cakes, puddings, and ice cream – they would be astounded. The common belief was that you had to live on apples and lettuce and not a lot else. One woman actually came to a workshop to find out more and said, 'Oh I thought it was going to be ten ways to peel a banana.' But raw food's time has come, and thanks to the dozens of high quality raw recipe books and internet sites around now, people are seeing how interesting and varied a raw diet can be.

Look at anyone who has followed a raw food diet consistently for a few years or more, has done their share of detoxing, purged a few inner demons, sloughed away some dead cells, and is on the road to optimum health. See how they glow with an inner radiance and vitality no amount of expensive beauty products can achieve. See the way they are so comfortable in their bodies, with a natural confidence that is incredibly attractive. See how they fully inhabit themselves, how they have a brighter, a more whole aura which is very affirming and healing to be around. Have a look at some of the raw movies on YouTube, the online movie channel, and you'll see what I mean.

So how do you get some of that magnetic charisma for yourself? Well first of all it has to be said that it does take years of dedication. Going raw for a short while isn't hard at all, but if you want to reap the full benefits, keep at it year on year and you'll be amazed as the old layers of yourself peel away, revealing the nakedly raw gloriously true you! It's a very liberating process. And it involves far more than just dietary changes, but encompasses a whole outlook on life - regular exercise, holistic therapies, helpful cleansing techniques and most importantly a shift in consciousness. Eating the raw way, nature's way, is one of affirmation, abundance, joy and vitality, and it's only going to work if you feed your mind the same high quality foods as your body, focus relentlessly on the positive, and try at all times to make the world a better place for you and everyone around you, thereby healing our beautiful planet. Honestly, there is nothing more sexy than an inner knowing that you are following your path, living true to your heart, and fulfilling your mission to create a more peaceful, loving world. The closer to nature you are, the more tuned into your body and the planet, the more you exude a wild, liberated fecund energy that is very intriguing to people and will draw them to you.

So you've been listening to your body and energising your life, and you've attracted a delicious mate, what are you going to feed them? Making food together is always a good start. Raw food preparation is very sensual. Roll up your sleeves and get stuck in there. Use your hands to toss the salad; use your fingers to scrape the jug; really massage that kale, knead that raw cookie dough and whip that cashew cream. Lots of licking fingers and feeding each other tasters off spoons works wonders to get the libido going.

- Maca is the number one aphrodisiacal food. With a not unpleasant, malty kind of taste, it is easy to add to most kinds of sweet dishes. Try some in your porridge or your yoghurt, sprinkle it on your cereal, add it to smoothies and fruit puddings, or make a spread with it and plaster it over your sprouted bread and dehydrated crackers. A simple summer recipe is to blend up one tablespoon of maca with a punnet of strawberries, a banana, and a splash of natural sweetener such as agave nectar. It is brilliant for extra energy and stamina – it provides a calm, centred and long lasting boost. It is a powerful hormone balancer, so restores the body's natural libido.

- Everyone loves chocolate but wait until you try it in its raw naked form, you will be blown away. It contains natural chemical compounds which boost serotonin levels and produce a real natural high. And of course, it helps the body to produce feel good hormones which are a great natural aphrodisiac. Try one of the sublime raw chocolate bars that are starting to appear in wholefood stores, and are sugar-free, wheat-free and dairy-free. Or even better, track down some cacao nibs and make your own. Making chocolate is like therapy – the aromas and the textures are incredibly sensual and very healing. Throw some maca in the mix and wow! Guaranteed fun.

- Maybe you are more of a savouries person? The raw fooder's favourite snack food is nori rolls. Get some raw nori sheets (not the toasted ones) and cram with creamy dips like hemp seed hummus, almond mayonnaise, or cacaomole (guacamole with extra chocolate in, really, it works). Sprinkle in some fresh wild herbs and locally sourced greens like rocket and spinach, layer in some alfalfa sprouts and roll. Share with your partner, one end each. Packed with minerals, this kind of food is very strengthening, and somehow there's something very sexy about bits of avocado spilling out of your mouth and dribbling down your chin. Nori rolls can't be eaten politely - you have to abandon yourself to them and that's all part of the fun.

■ One of the simplest and most effective aphrodisiacs is a good old-fashioned brew. Some herbs have been used for centuries for their nurturing and reviving properties. A cup of herbal tea after your dinner is sure to have you heading straight for the bedroom - in fact you might not even make it that far....Try one of the blended brands on the market, or look out for herbs such as yohimbe, damiana or bala.

Now excuse me, after all that I'm off to find myself a handsome raw man who has so much energy and stamina he can keep going all night and still be up in the morning to feed me exotic fruit and freshly made juice - or even some more chocolate...

■ Superfoods

I love superfoods. I eat them every day, and have done for nearly two decades. I don't know how I could survive without them – sure, I would still be alive, but I think I can state categorically that I would not be as happy and energetic as I am without them, and I certainly wouldn't be leading such a joyful and abundant life. They provide me with that edge, that get-up and go, which helps me deal with the demands of motherhood, and still have energy for myself. As a breastfeeding mother, I could be sure my high nutritional requirements were being met. And when my children are fussy and push away the green vegetables on their plates, I can rest assured they will get their greens one way or another.

Although most people have heard of superfoods, there is some confusion over what the term actually means. I would classify them as natural plant foods which are exceptionally high in nutrition and thereby provide the body with increased energy. Broccoli and blueberries are not superfoods. They may be very healthy food choices, but they don't have the super-charged density and vitality of true superfoods. True superfoods really can transform you into a super-being. Because all the vitamins, minerals, amino acids, enzymes, fatty acids and more, are so packed in, a little goes along way. A lot of energy is saved on the digestion process, and if taken correctly and the body is functioning well, they are easily absorbed and assimilated, so providing an instant boost. Superfoods are generally superior to supplements because they are literally a wholefood. Anything that has been synthesised in a laboratory or chemically isolated is not going to send the body as strong and clear a message as a natural plant food which has simply been dried or powdered. This is one reason why superfoods are gaining popularity so quickly: you definitely notice when you take them, and you can really feel the difference.

Many superfoods grow in poor, isolated, but unspoilt regions like Peru and Tibet. They are well known in their native countries, and have been eaten for centuries by the indigenous populations, but no-one has properly looked into their nutritional benefits and properties before. With the demand for healthy food options increasing in the West, and the wholefoods market being one of the biggest retail growth sectors, much research is now being done in the search for innovative new products, and many amazing new foods are being discovered and brought to us here in the UK. So you may read on and think, but I've never heard of any of these foods! That's because many of them have only been easily available here for a year or two, sometimes even less. But word is spreading fast about their amazing health benefits and you can bet you'll soon be seeing goji berries next to the Maltesers packets on supermarket checkouts.

The most well-known superfoods currently are the algaes (spirulina, Klamath Lake blue-green algae, and chlorella), bee pollen and aloe vera. Wheatgrass is also widely recognised for its health benefits, but people are less likely to have it regularly because ideally it is consumed freshly juiced. Some of the newer ones which have been around a couple of years now are cacao, maca and goji berries. And then we have the really new kids on the block like suma, camu camu, purple corn, noni juice, crystal manna and more.... There are a lot of superfood blends on the market too; where anything from 10-100 high potency foods are powdered together. Basically, I would say that old adage is true, 'you get what you pay for'. If one brand is less expensive than another, it probably has cheaper ingredients and fillers in it. Generally, all these blends are quite costly and not optimum because they have been put through a greater degree of processing to reach you. Many of them contain a large number of different ingredients, and it can be overwhelming for the body to be bombarded with complicated messages in this way. No superfood is a bad superfood, and they can all be helpful, but some more than others.

It is very hard to compare the different qualities of the superfoods that we use; it's a bit like trying to compare a carrot with a parsnip or a cabbage. They each have their own distinctive individual character, so people often have a particular aversion to one but get on really well with another. The correct dosage is also hard to predict. It is always best to start off with a little, say half a teaspoon, at least for the first couple of days. You may notice a reaction straight away and like it – in which case up the dose! If you don't notice anything, you probably need more, so again, gradually up the dose until you start feeling the effects. If you notice a detox reaction such as an old complaint flaring up, spots or tummy troubles, this is just the body rebalancing, so stick with a minimum maintenance dose and after a few days you should have shifted some stuff and be feeling much better.

- Algae is the oldest life-form on earth; 'primordial food'. When we eat algae we connect with that really ancient energy. It is a very deep healing, but gentle food, and a good one to start with. There are three classes of algae widely available: chlorella, spirulina, and Klamath Lake blue-green algae. Spirulina is the best source of protein, but Klamath Lake is on the whole nutritionally superior. The Klamath Lake is in Oregon, it is a nutrient trap, and the algae that grows in it is one of the finest foods available to us. It is nutritionally complete, which means it contains absolutely every known nutrient the body needs. Not only that, they are in the ideal ratios for bioavailability. If you had to sit down and design the perfect food, blue-green algae would be hard to beat.

- Bee pollen is also a complete food. If you were stranded on a desert island with nothing but bee pollen and water, theoretically you would have everything you needed (although I don't think anyone's ever tested it out!) Bee pollen is a bit of a misnomer, because although it is collected by bees on their legs, it actually comes from flowers. It's a great one for kids because it has a naturally sweet taste, like honey; my boys have it on their cereal every morning. It is very energising, good for those days when you have a dozen errands to run before school pick-up, and you need to be buzzing around all day.

- Aloe vera comes from a cactus plant and is usually drunk like a juice. The quality of aloe vera on the market is very variable – if it tastes like water it probably is just that. Aloe is a truly amazing plant, as well as having a strong nutritional profile it has anti-viral and anti-microbial properties, and is a natural painkiller. Much research is being conducted in the UK on aloe at the moment, due to its widely reported benefits with both skin conditions like eczema and psoriasis, and gut problems such as Irritable Bowel Syndrome (IBS) and colitis. Because of its immune boosting properties, it is taken by many people suffering from immune disorders from asthma to lupus and cancer. And if all that wasn't enough, it is also popular with those suffering with joint problems, particularly sports people and the elderly.

- Wheatgrass comes tops for detoxifying and cleansing as it is exceptionally high in chlorophyll. Chlorophyll has a very similar composition to human blood: you could call it plant blood, and as such, it is very healing. It is best consumed freshly juiced, for which you need a good quality juicer, or you can find it at many juice bars; the powdered versions don't really compare. It is one of the most potent foods you will ever find; very good at balancing blood sugar, and used to treat serious diseases such as cancer and diabetes.

- Cacao is known as the food of the gods. Native to South America, it is the bean that cocoa solids are made from, so is literally raw chocolate. It is one of the highest dietary sources of magnesium and sulphur, as well as containing an off the chart level of antioxidants. It is full of natural chemicals which boost the mood and elevate energy levels, so providing an unbeatable natural high. Plus (unlike wheatgrass), it tastes wonderful – a luxurious sweet treat you can pig out on, and then feel heavenly afterwards, surely the answer to every woman's dreams...

- Maca is a Peruvian root vegetable which is most commonly found in powdered form. It is a great source of protein and minerals such as calcium and iron. It is a hormone balancer, so is great for Pre-Menstrual Tension (PMT), as a natural form of Hormone Replacement Therapy (HRT), and is used to treat osteoporosis. It is also the number one for pregnant and breastfeeding mothers, to help boost energy and stamina. It's even a natural aphrodisiac so it's good for making babies too.

- Goji berries are perhaps the most accessible superfood. They come from one of the purest places on earth, the Himalayan Mountains, and are the most nutrient dense fruit on the planet. They come to us dried, like raisins, but they taste far better. They contain all the essential amino acids, so they're a great source of protein, as well as being one of the highest natural sources of beta-carotene and vitamin C. Children love them: we eat them all day long, in our cereal for breakfast, in trail mixes, in smoothies, in puddings, cakes, salads, or just as they are. In China they say the only side effect to eating too many gojis is laughing too much.

So, I hope this introduction to the irresistible world of superfoods has whetted your appetite. There are so many to try, they couldn't be easier to incorporate into your existing diet, and they are absolutely, undeniably, beneficial - I truly believe that there's something wonderful there for everyone to discover.

■ Supporting techniques

Eating raw is by no means the be all and end all of good health. There are plenty of unhealthy raw fooders around to prove that point. A lot of people try and go '100% raw' and then after a year or two, they say it can't be done, because it didn't work for them. It's very common for people to go raw and for the first few months feel fantastic, better than they have done in years. But if eating raw is not part of a whole lifestyle package, it's impossible to sustain at that level. That's why I believe it's important at the beginning to keep it in balance: see it as a long term goal, maybe five or ten years. There are no doubt a few exceptions around, but generally no-one manages to go 100% raw and then stay there. Sometimes problems surface quite quickly; other times it can take years for long suppressed issues to arise.

The key factor in all this is your state of mind. Where is your consciousness at? Raw foods are so full of vitality, they make one feel much more alive, and more present in the moment. We open up to that natural state of joy, love and abundance that is our birthright. But it is very hard in our culture to sustain that vibration. Raw foods have a very high vibrational level; superfoods even higher. So when we eat like this, we are opening ourselves up to these levels. And every single one of us has issues that need working on, fears and self-doubts that block our energy. So if we are not actively engaged in personal development, if 'being the change that we want to see in the world' is not our motivating factor, then raw foods are not going to work for us. We are going to need to eat foods of a lower vibration to help us feel grounded and in our bodies and not spaced out. For most people who are drawn to raw foods, creating a better world is part of their global view. But often it is just one thread in a busy and complex life.

Holding together the day-to-day responsibilities of a career, home and family are the preoccupying concerns for most of us, and the food we eat needs to support us in that, give us energy to fulfill our potential and to make the most out of life. Hence I emphasise the importance of 'being where you're at' with raw foods, and not pushing it to extremes, because that is not holistic. If you're stressing over whether to eat some food that maybe isn't an optimum health choice, I say eat it; far better to enjoy it rather than create stress in your life, or even worse, repress and deny your instincts. Our thoughts have the power to shape our lives; be mindful of yours.

Everyone knows that exercise is equally vital to a healthy lifestyle. If you're too busy to fit any into your daily routine, there is something out of balance in your life. If you're pressed for time, rebounding is great; just five minutes can tone the whole body and help stimulate the lymphatic system. Rebounding is basically just bouncing on a mini-trampoline. It's fun to do to music, or even while you're watching TV. It places no strain on the joints, boosts circulation, and improves muscle tone. I often stop for rebounding sessions between writing chapters to loosen things up and keep the brain fresh. Yoga is very popular among raw food devotees: the two have a naturally symbiotic relationship. Both are about tuning into one's body, achieving a union between the higher and lower self. Many yoga students turn to raw foods because they find it helps them get more flexible, and go further into their meditation; many raw fooders discover yoga as an ideal way to keep vibrant and attuned. Whatever exercise suits you best, swimming, walking, or cycling to work every day, if you consider it as vital a part of your daily routine as taking a shower and brushing your teeth, your body will love you for it.

Water is the most vital requirement for human life. The purer the water we drink, the better we can assimilate nutrients and flush out toxins. The quality of the water you drink is more important than any of the food you put into your body. You can eat the healthiest foods on the planet, but if you are not drinking enough water, your body will not be able to absorb and utilise the nutrients from the food. We use Pure H2O water, the purest water available. The water is put through a unique patented process of reverse osmosis filtration and deionisation. Reverse osmosis is a process developed by NASA which squeezes water through a semi-permeable membrane under pressure, rejecting impurities such as heavy metals, viruses, and hormones. The membrane is so fine, only hydrogen and oxygen molecules can pass through. Next, the water goes through a deionisation process, which removes more impurities, and finally it passes through a granular activated carbon filter, which has great abilities to absorb many of the organic contaminants found in water. The purity of water is measured by TDS – the total dissolved solids the water contains. UK tap water contains an average of 500 parts per million; jug filters can reduce that to about 425 ppm. Bottled mineral ranges from 150 ppm to up to 600 ppm, but pure H_2O water contains only 2 ppm TDS. This water is sold and recommended by most of the UK's leading health food stores including Fresh and Wild, Planet Organic, and Infinity Foods.

I am a great believer in colonics and enemas. Some people dismiss them as unnatural, but I feel there is so much about our modern lifestyles that is unnatural that these deep cleansing techniques are vital for keeping our bodies in balance. To me, cleaning my colon is as basic as cleaning my outer body: I couldn't go for more than a few days without a bath or a shower before I started feeling dirty, and if I go too long without colon cleansing I feel a similar unclean feeling. We accumulate so much waste matter in our guts; one colonic hydrotherapist told me that the most common substance found is mother's milk. Another told me you could have a colonic every day for a year before you stopped pulling stuff out; we produce so much waste matter continually. We are literally carrying around a lifetime's debris inside us. I recommend doing enemas at least once or twice a month, and having a colonic at least once or twice a year. I find the most beneficial times for cleansing are around the equinoxes and solstice, so choose to have them then if you can. Colonics are performed by registered practitioners in hygienic surroundings. They are more thorough than enemas, and clean higher up the colon. Enemas can be self-administered in your own home. They may feel strange at first, but with a bit of practice they become easy, quick and not at all uncomfortable. Enema bags can easily be purchased online. I like to do two in a row; the first with just plain water and some essential oils such as lavender, eucalyptus or peppermint, for cleansing; then I do a second containing nutritional substances which can be absorbed directly through the colon walls. I usually put in a probiotic to help build healthy gut bacteria, and MSM, naturally occurring sulphur crystals, which assists with absorption and increases overall body flexibility. Then I add a superfood such as aloe vera, spirulina, barleygrass or noni juice, as well as some hemp or flax oil to get an extra dose of EFAs. Each enema takes about twenty minutes in total (I have an enema information video on YouTube if you want more information). It doesn't matter how healthily we eat, our bodies are continually stressed by pollutants in the environment and in our lifestyles, and it seems to me that enemas are one of the simplest and most effective ways of dealing with the toll 21st century living takes on our bodies. They are excellent ways of building digestive fire too, as retaining the water strengthens the muscles in the colon walls and teaches the gut to work more efficiently. So many people in our culture suffer from problems like IBS and colitis, which could often be easily remedied by a colon cleansing programme. Our guts have been weakened by decades of wrong eating and a build-up of debris and waste matter, no wonder they can't cope any more with the demands put on them. It doesn't matter how healthily you are eating if the cell walls in the gut are so clogged up you are not absorbing any nutrients.

As we become more conscious about the foods we put in our bodies, we begin to wonder about all the other things our bodies come into contact with too. There are an incredible number of pollutants in the environment, many of which can be reduced very simply. Here's just a few of the ways you can 'detox your world' (as a good friend of mine once said):

■ Use more natural products on our hair and skin, not ones full of unpronounceable chemicals. At the time of writing there is only one skincare range in the UK made specifically with all raw ingredients – Raw Gaia. And there are many more excellent animal-free and organic products around. Look for ingredients like aloe vera, lavender or rose oil, hemp, MSM, and cacao butter, and check that what you are buying contains significant quantities of these special plant products, not just a token splash.

■ Buy clothes and linen made with natural fibres, organic cotton or hemp if possible. The chemicals used in growing cotton are some of the biggest pollutants on the planet, and cause massive health problems for the growers and pickers. Organic is more expensive, but it is becoming more accessible, and feels wonderful on the skin. Hemp is one of the most durable fabrics around, and is amazingly soft to wear. It is good for the soil, uses little water, and needs no pesticides. Again, nowadays there is a growing range of hemp clothes made by young ethical designers - you can even buy hemp lingerie.

■ Be aware of electromagnetic pollution, try to minimize the use of electrical equipment, and use protection devices wherever possible. I believe that the invisible pollution we are all bombarded with in the 21st century is one of the biggest potential health hazards we face. No-one yet knows the consequences of the extensive use of computers, mobile phones, cordless phones, satellite navigation systems and so on. Undoubtedly all these things make our lives much easier and more pleasurable, but they also potentially have hidden side effects. Leading a holistic lifestyle involves keeping all these devices in balance and using protective materials like crystals, or ones which have been specifically devised to protect against electromagnetic pollution like tachyon devices and plasmonic plates. Although your inner cynic might not be convinced there is enough evidence that these things actually work, I feel it is better to be over-cautious and invest in whichever gadgets you are drawn to.

■ Avoid unnecessary antibiotics, vaccinations and other pharmaceutical products, and seek out natural therapies like homeopathy, flower essences and acupuncture. Please don't get me started on the horrors of the pharmaceutical industry. If you want more information, a good place to start is www.newstarget.com, an independent US website which contains a real wealth of information on natural health, nutrition and more. Many of the illnesses which we take medication for can be just as easily corrected with natural remedies. When we get ill, it is our body's way of clearing stuff out, and telling us to slow down and rest a bit. Allopathic medicine merely suppresses symptoms, and does not help the body detoxify fully. Indeed, conventional medicine tends to weaken the immune system because it does not allow the body to do the work itself, but does the job of fighting disease for it. Alternative therapies on the other hand, support the body in releasing toxins and make it stronger and healthier in the long term. And don't wait until you are ill to have a treatment; invest in your health continually. It is much more enjoyable having a preventative massage or Reiki session than having to drag yourself off somewhere for a consultation when you are feeling run down and terrible.

■ Invest in air ionisers and purifiers, and keep windows open as much as possible to ensure circulation of fresh air. If you have windows closed all the time, this leads to a build up of carbon dioxide; open windows allow oxygen to circulate, making you feel more energized and alert. In the winter, try and avoid having the central heating on unnecessarily; it is very dehydrating and contributes to creating a sluggish system. Far better to make your internal fire work a bit by feeling the cold, than allowing it to get lazy by adjusting the temperature artificially.

There are many easy-to-practice home remedies to assist the body in releasing toxins. Once you've been on a high raw diet for a few months, your body is going to start releasing a lot of old 'stuff'. People usually find it is around the three month mark that things start to get moving for them. Often, people can take up a healthy habit for three months, but when it gets to the point where stuff is starting to shift for them, if they don't feel supported in making the appropriate changes in their lives, they fall back into old patterns. That is why detoxification techniques are so important, to enable the whole body to move forward, rather than just focussing on the one area like diet and then the rest of the body struggles to keep up.

There are lots of ways to ensure you have beautiful, radiant, naturally healthy skin. Your skin will love you if you have regular steams or saunas, which help open the pores and release toxins. Steam rooms are better because they are wet heat; saunas are dry heat which is more dehydrating. Whichever you take, make sure to drink plenty of water during the session. Skin brushing helps to stimulate the lymphatic system, remove dead skin cells, and also leaves your skin looking great. You can buy a dry bristle brush from a health food store or chemist, simply brush towards the heart, with long, hard strokes, before showering. Cold baths and showers are amazing; I have been taking cold showers for around fifteen years, and cold baths for around five years. I never notice the cold now, and I am sure this is largely because this daily boost to my circulation means I have built up a strong inner fire. The best way to shower is to run the shower cold first for as long as you can stand it; then have a usual hot shower and wash; then do alternate cold/hot/cold/hot/cold to end, always finishing with the cold. Cold baths are even more stimulating: after you've had your usual soak in a hot tub, drain the water out and remain in the bath. Then refill the bath with cold water, and stay in as long as you can, submerging your head and body completely if possible. Not only does this really get your system working full power, it's great for the mind too, as you're going beyond the usual limitations you set yourself and breaking down barriers to what you believe is possible. Your head tells you, 'I can't do this, it's too cold!', but if you push it and don't listen to that voice, you realise that you can do it, and really it isn't that bad after all. So often in life it's our belief that we can't do something that stops us achieving it and techniques like this help us to create a positive attitude and inner mastery of situations.

Bathing in Epsom salts is an excellent way to remove toxins from the body; the salts draw acidic wastes out through the pores of the skin and they also have a high magnesium content, a mineral many of us are lacking in. You need to put about 500 g in a bath, and they are easily found in chemists. Another simple home remedy for drawing out toxicity is the use of castor oil packing: castor oil has anti-microbial and anti-bacterial properties and due to its full spectrum light content is excellent at pulling rubbish out of the body. Again, castor oil is cheap and easy to find in most chemists. Simply soak an old flannel or muslin or some special packing fabric in the oil, and place on the area where you want to achieve results. Liver-packing is very beneficial, also packing on your lungs when you have a chest infection can be very helpful. Place a hot water bottle on top of the pack so the heat can help with the process. Settle down with a book or in front of a film for a couple of hours, or wear overnight while you sleep. Castor oil stains, so wear old clothes and sheets, or use plastic bags to cover the packing fabric and avoid it getting in contact with other materials. I love castor oil packing; it is wonderfully nourishing, nurturing and soothing.

Finally, I highly recommend the work of Barbara Wren, and the College of Natural Nutrition which she founded. Barbara was a nurse who suffered from anorexia nervosa when she was younger, and ME (Myalgic Encephalopathy or Chronic Fatigue Syndrome) later in life. She had four children, and took her own journey to find optimum health. Her philosophy incorporates a high raw diet, as well as naturopathic techniques like castor oil packing and enemas, and observing the cycles of the moon and the sun. I love her methods particularly because they are generally so low-cost and easy to do, but have such far-reaching effects on our health.

◼ The journey

People are attracted to raw foods for many different reasons. Most commonly, they just want more energy; some want to lose weight, others to correct a medical condition like IBS or clear up a skin condition. Some have a serious health challenge such as cancer, others are perfectly healthy and want to stay that way. But whatever your motivation, raw foods are in themselves a journey, and I believe, a very spiritual journey. Eating raw opens you up to your true self, it helps you to look honestly at your life and the people in it. It's a common complaint among rawfooders that they find it hard to tell a lie! Being raw is a process of stripping away the layers of cooked food addiction; the fears, doubts and insecurities we have about ourselves are revealed bare, and at first it can feel quite exposed. But the more we get accustomed to being in our raw, naked state, and shed those false skins of protection, the more liberated we feel. This kind of liberation is like medicine; it might not always taste good, but it sure makes you feel better.

When I look at my own personal growth through raw foods it astounds me. I never worry about my weight now, whereas that was a major preoccupation throughout my teenage years. I always eat as much as I want and I never feel overweight. I have limitless supplies of energy, and need on average only six hours sleep a night. I don't get tired despite my 110 mph lifestyle - three children, a thriving business, and a busy social life. Because I feed myself only the highest quality plant foods this amazing planet has to offer, I love my body and it rarely lets me down. My thoughts always tend towards the positive, because my food is so full of life energy so am I. Sure, I have challenges and crises in my life, that's all part of being human, but I now have the confidence to know I will get through them, and a faith in the universe that leads me to understand everything happens for a reason, and there is always a valuable lesson to be learnt in every situation. I am relentlessly happy and upbeat, almost to the point of being annoying, and feel gratitude in my heart for my life and all the amazing people in it. I am so at peace with myself, I feel the joy bubbling over on a daily basis. And so I attract fewer and fewer people into my life who judge me, disrespect me, or misunderstand me. Instead I draw in people who appreciate me and recognise my contribution to humanity. The more I surround myself with these amazing people, the happier I get, and the more beautiful beings I pull in!

This can work for you because you are eating foods that have a pure and harmonious energy, so you too start to create more of these energies in your life. When you are living in the present, in the moment, you are tuned in to yourself and your life's higher purpose and miracles start to manifest themselves daily. It can just be little things like making it to the car one minute before the traffic warden comes round the corner, or a friend turning up with just the book/ CD/ raw cookies that you had been thinking about. But it can also be major life changes like finding a new partner, taking a new career path, or moving house. It's a fundamental universal law at work: the more bliss you find in your food, the more bliss you create in yourself, the more bliss you attract into your life.

Raw foods were an integral part of the journey to get me to this space. And no matter what the reality of your initial motivation for going raw, this is where it will lead you if you follow the path; to a place of love, joy, abundance and vitality. It's what I call Raw Magic. But that's a whole other story...

■ Sample menus

Here are some ideas to get you started and give you a good idea of what is possible on the raw diet. If you follow these menus for two weeks, you'll be so full of good food you won't be going hungry, but you're also likely to have more energy than ever and feel fantastic. Most people find that after a few months, weeks or even days of eating good quality raw food meals their appetites start to diminish and they are happier with simpler dishes and smaller meals, but if you're seeking to banish the cooked food cravings and keep fully raw, following these menus will be really helpful guidelines for you.

* denotes that there is a recipe in the book for this dish.

■ Day one:
Breakfast – Cereal *
Mid-morning – 1 Chocolate Brownie *
Lunch – Reuben's Guacamole *, carrot sticks, fresh rocket in
    Red Pepper Dressing *
Mid-afternoon – Seasonal fruit
Tea – Spicy Almond Burgers * with Red Pepper Ketchup *
    and Fennel and Leek Salad *

- **Day two:**
  Breakfast – Breakfast Pudding *
  Mid-morning – 2 Sand Biscuits *
  Lunch – Beetroot Soup *
  Mid-afternoon – Courgette Crisps * and Zachary's Dip *
  Tea – Red Cabbage Salad * and Mashed Parsnips *

- **Day three:**
  Breakfast – Fresh juice made with 1/2 cucumber, 2 sticks celery and
      1/2 lemon
  Mid-morning – Dulse Crisps * and Coriander Chutney *
  Lunch – Rye Essene Bread *, alfalfa sprouts and Cashew Cream
      Cheese *
  Mid-afternoon – Seasonal fruit
  Tea – 'Chicken' Salad *

- **Day four:**
  Breakfast – Can't Beta It *
  Mid-morning – Raw Chocolate *
  Lunch – Seasonal green salad leaves and sunflower sprouts
      in Creamy Cucumber Dressing *
  Mid-afternoon – 2 Oatcakes * and pumpkin seed butter
  Tea – Chilli *

- **Day five:**
  Breakfast – Cereal *
  Mid-morning – Seasonal fruit
  Lunch – Walnut PČté * and carrot and pepper sticks
  Mid-afternoon – Fresh juice made with 1/2 cucumber, 2 celery sticks,
  1 apple
  Tea – Dahl *

- **Day six:**
  Breakfast – Miso Bread * and tahini
  Mid-morning – Maca Balls *
  Lunch – Nori rolls stuffed with Parsley Dip *, cucumber sticks and
      alfalfa sprouts
  Mid-afternoon – Seasonal fruit
  Tea – Sausages * and Carrot Ketchup * and fresh corn salad and
      avocado dressed in Tapenade *

- **Day seven:**
  Breakfast – Gorgeous Goji Pudding *
  Mid-morning – 2 Lovely Biscuits *
  Lunch – Broccoli Bliss *
  Mid-afternoon – Green Leather *
  Tea – Tempura * and baby leaf spinach with lentil sprouts and
    Sweet Chilli Sauce *

- **Day eight:**
  Breakfast – Cereal *
  Mid-morning – 2 Supersweeties *
  Lunch – Fantastic Fennel Soup *
  Mid-afternoon – Sweet Potato Crisps * and Date Chutney *
  Tea – Big plate mixed salad leaves and olives dressed
    with Avo Pesto *

- **Day nine:**
  Breakfast – Breakfast Pudding *
  Mid-morning – Fresh juice made with 4 sticks celery and 1 apple
  Lunch – Porcini mushrooms and pesto *
  Mid-afternoon – 2 Carrot Cakes *
  Tea – Fattoush * and Chips *

- **Day ten:**
  Breakfast – Cereal *
  Mid-morning – Seasonal fresh fruit
  Lunch – My Favourite Things *
  Mid-afternoon – 1 Chocolate Brownie *
  Tea – Pizza Peppers *

- **Day eleven:**
  Breakfast – Can't Beta It *
  Mid-morning – 2 Quinoa Crackers *
  Lunch – Mediterranean Stuffed Tomatoes *
  Mid-afternoon – Salad Bar *
  Tea – Satay Sweet Potatoes * and Simple Salad *

- **Day twelve:**
  Breakfast – Fresh juice made with 2 sticks celery, 2 carrots and 1 cm (1/2 in) ginger
  Mid-morning – 2 Flapjacks *
  Lunch – Nori rolls stuffed with Hemp Seed Hummus *, lettuce leaves and alfalfa sprouts
  Mid-afternoon – 2 Maca Balls *
  Tea - Sweetheart Salad *

- **Day thirteen:**
  Breakfast – Rye Essene Bread * with Jam *
  Mid-morning – Fresh juice made with 2 carrots, 1 apple and 2 sticks celery
  Lunch – Cabbage Medley *
  Mid-afternoon – 2 Lisa's Raw Indian Bars *
  Tea – Parsnip Rice * and Eat Your Greens *

- **Day fourteen:**
  Breakfast – Best Ever Chocolate Pudding *
  Mid-morning – 2 Apple Cashew Cookies *
  Lunch – Oakleaf lettuce with Pineapple Dressing *
  Mid-afternoon – Plantain Chips *
  Tea – Thai Red Curry *

■ Sprouting

There are many different sprouting gadgets on the market which you may choose to invest in, but personally I have always stuck with the old fashioned jam jar method. I use a one litre size glass jar for smaller quantities of sprouts. If I am doing large amounts, e.g. a batch of buckwheat for dehydrating, I use a large Pyrex, ceramic or glass bowl. Most sprouts simply need soaking in the purest water available, then rinsing once a day. In very hot weather you may need to rinse twice a day to prevent them going off. I rinse mine by filling the receptacle they are in with pure water, swishing them around with my hands, then draining them off in a sieve.

Sprouts are an amazing food for several reasons. They are the ultimate in fresh food, so you know exactly how they have been grown and that they are still full of their life force. Sprouting increases the nutritional content drastically: proteins, minerals, vitamins and enzymes increase and become more bioavailable. When you sprout grains, the starches which many people are intolerant to are converted into natural sugars, so most people who have a gluten problem are fine with sprouted wheat, spelt, rye and oats. Finally sprouting is incredibly economical as the raw seeds, beans and grains cost pennies and you can produce huge platefuls of sprouts for next to nothing.

The following are the sprouts that are commonly used throughout this book.

Aduki, mung, green lentil, brown lentil: soak 60 g/2 oz for 8-12 hrs, sprout 3-5 days. These are among the easiest things to sprout. You can use them individually or make a mix and sprout them in the same jar together.

Alfalfa: soak 1-2 tbsp for 4-8 hrs, sprout 7 days. A raw staple, a small amount of seeds makes a massive amount of sprouts.

Buckwheat: soak 150 g/5 oz for 5 hrs, sprout 3 days. Buckwheat needs careful attention as it has a tendency to go slimy. Give the seeds a good rinse before soaking and another after. Don't soak for more than 5 hrs; you get better results if you rinse twice a day.

Chick pea: soak 150 g/5 oz for 8-12 hrs, sprout 3 days. Easy to do, don't let the tails get longer than the bean or they will taste woody.

Quinoa: soak 120 g/4 oz for 4-8 hrs, sprout 3-5 days. Quite tricky to sprout, needs lots of attention, rinse twice a day.

Sunflower: soak 60 g/2 oz for 4-8 hrs, sprout 1 -3 days. Don't over sprout these or they taste bitter.

Wheat, spelt, oats and rye: soak 90 g/3 oz for 8-12 hrs, sprout 3-5 days. Sprouted grains are used for making breads, or make a filling, tasty and nutritious addition to salads.

■ Kitchen notes

The availability of raw food ingredients is growing steadily. It's very exciting to see all these new, previously unheard of products come into the country. Be adventurous, and you will be astounded at the endless amount of new meals you can come up with.

■ Blenders

I have a Vitamix, and where I say blender in a recipe, that's what I've used. The Vitamix is an amazing machine, and revolutionised what I can do in the kitchen. It is basically a very high-powered blender, capable of blending just about anything. It also does a good job of grinding nuts, seeds, grains, beans, etc. However it is very expensive (at the time of printing, it retails for about £500). It's a great investment, if you can afford it, and invaluable for easy and efficient raw food preparation. I haven't tested these recipes with a standard blender, but I know that your average machine would find some of the combinations hard work. If things aren't churning up nicely for you, try putting your mixture in the food processor with the S-blade in. Sometimes this on its own will do the trick, but for a smoother finish, put the mixture back in the blender and it should be able to handle it better. You can also try using a hand-held blender. These can be more efficient at achieving a thorough blending when a standard blender just isn't up to it.

■ Carob, mesquite and lucuma

We have been able to buy raw carob powder in this country for a few years now. Otherwise I recommend the organic brands manufactured by Rapunzel or Hambleden Herbs. I used to think they were raw; they're not, they're toasted rather than roasted, but they're very good quality nonetheless. You can also buy whole carob pods which make a delicious healthy sweet snack.

Siesta make fantastic carob bars, which are wheat-free, sugar-free, dairy-free, hydrogenated fat-free, as well as actually tasting nice (unlike some brands). We use their carob flakes, which are wonderful for sprinkling as a garnish, or in cookie mixtures. At Christmas and Easter, they make seasonal goodies like eggs and Father Christmases, which the children love.

Mesquite is another powdered sweetener which also comes from a pod. It is from the same family as carob. Just to confuse you, there is one variety of raw carob on the market which is called Algorroba and actually tastes more like mesquite than the usual Spanish carob. Lucuma is a powdered Peruvian fruit which has a wonderful shortbread flavour. You can substitute mesquite or lucuma for carob in any recipe, or try using them in combination.

■ Dates and dried fruit

I love fresh dates; they're one of my preferred methods of sweetening a dish. Dates are so nutritious that in the desert, people survive for long periods on a diet of little else but dates and camel milk! The best ones are the Iranian dates which aren't too expensive and are raw and fresh. Many greengrocers and wholefood stores stock them. They come in cardboard boxes, weigh about 500g, and are usually kept in the fridge. If you can get them, I really recommend fresh dates over dried dates. Dried dates have usually been heat treated and aren't so nutritionally potent. If you are using dried dates in a recipe, always soak them for twenty minutes to one hour first. Drink the soaking water afterwards, it's yummy.

Most dried fruit is heated to various degrees and is best eaten sparingly because of its high sugar content. Buy only dried fruits which are unsulphured and have no added vegetable oils or sugar coatings.

■ Dehydrators

Basically a box with a fan and heating element, dehydrators are like a raw oven, heating food at very low temperatures to preserve the nutritional status and enzymatic activity. The most popular dehydrator is the Excalibur because the trays are a good size and easily accessible, and it has a variable temperature control. There are some cheaper ones around but they are not so user-friendly.

Some dehydrators have variable temperature controls, and some do not. We have not given any temperatures in this book: the standard temperature for dehydrating raw foods is 38°C/100°F.

■ Dried tomatoes

I generally make my own dried tomatoes by blending some fresh in a jug and then drying them in the dehydrator until they're crispy. It doesn't take long, and it's so much cheaper than buying shop ones, which often have salt or preservatives added. If you don't have a dehydrator, look for the ones which come dry in packets rather than the ones in jars covered in oil, as these are far more economical. Soak shop-bought ones in water for at least twenty minutes, up to an hour, before you use them.

■ Grain coffee

There are many different brands of grain coffee on the market, such as Barleycup and Yannoh. They are not raw, but when used in combination with carob powder in a recipe, produce a wonderful deep chocolately taste.

■ Juicers

With most juicers it is generally a case of you get what you pay for. High street centrifugal juicers might seem like a good option when you are starting out but they have a number of drawbacks. They can be difficult to clean, and with the cheaper models you don't always get a lot of juice out of them. Gear juicers are a better investment because they produce more juice and have extended warranties so will last you longer. Twin gear juicers are the tops for making green juices out of vegetables like celery, cucumber and leafy greens. Single gear juicers juice fruits and vegetables efficiently and are the easiest to clean. Another advantage to gear juicers is that they can also be used with a homogenizing plate to make purées and nut butters. There are many different models of juicer available in the UK, rising in price to around £400; shop around, and see which one will suit your needs and your pocket.

■ Lecithin granules

Derived from soya, lecithin helps with the emulsification of fats so it is a good supplement to take with flax oil to aid the liver in absorption. It is also rich in phosphatidyl-choline, a good brain food.
Lecithin granules have a pleasant, almost cheesy flavour and are another simple and easy ingredient to sprinkle on your salads.

■ Psyllium husk powder

Psyllium is a root similar to plantain. The husks are sold in pharmacies and wholefood stores as a digestive aid. When soaked in water, they swell up and absorb the water, creating a sort of jelly, which acts as an intestinal broom. In raw food cuisine they act as an effective healthy, animal-free gelling agent. I prefer to use powdered husks as they give a smoother, less grainy result.

Nuts and seeds

Nuts are best used in moderation. For a start, most of the packaged nuts have been heat treated to varying degrees – cashews are guaranteed not to be raw, unless you buy the Sunfood ones imported from the USA. But nuts are quite hard work for the body to deal with, and if you eat too many they can leave you feeling sluggish and heavy. Consume large amounts on a regular basis (a common pitfall for raw food beginners) and you're going to congest your liver and make yourself sick. Have a shot of wheatgrass – if you feel sick, chances are you need to stay off the nuts for a while. As a general rule eat no more nuts in a day than you can hold in one fist.

Seeds are much gentler on the body than nuts, and more nutritionally dynamic. Sesame, pumpkin, sunflower and hemp are the main four. I generally try and soak my nuts and seeds first before I use them – if you forget it's not the end of the world, but it's a good habit to get into on a regular basis. On average, seeds need 4–8 hrs, nuts 8–12 hrs (because they're bigger). But even if you've only got twenty minutes, that's better than nothing. Soaking releases the enzyme inhibitors, making them more digestible and friendlier to the liver. And of course, it also makes them bigger as they swell up and absorb the water, so you're also getting more for your money.

Nut and seed butters

Only a few years ago, it was next to impossible to get raw nut and seed butters in the UK. Rapunzel tahini and white almond butter have been around for a while now, and are staples of a raw food cupboard; indispensable as a base for sauces and dressings, as well as a spread for crackers and breads. At the time of writing, you can also buy Omega Nutrition pumpkin seed butter and Carley's do a wide range of excellent raw nut butters, such as rainforest, pecan and hemp. There is also a range imported from America called Rejuvenative foods, made specifically for raw fooders, including pistachio, black sesame and hazelnut. Anything else you are better off steering clear of because the nuts or seeds have been roasted, making them difficult to digest, more mucus-forming, and hard work for the liver.

The raw ones aren't cheap, but are very high quality and so heavenly they are well worth the expense. Use them sparingly. Even raw nut butters are very congesting, and should be eaten as treats, not by the spoon (although we've all done it!).

■ Nutritional yeast flakes

Not a raw product, but rich in B vitamins and a delicious addition to raw savouries when used minimally, and favoured commonly for their cheesy taste. The yeast in the flakes is inactive, so they are suitable for use for people who have a yeast intolerance.

■ Oats

Nearly all oats grown commercially for sale in the UK are steamed to stabilize them. Oats go rancid easily, and without this treatment they would only be able to sit on shop shelves for weeks rather than years. Raw Living produce fresh oat groats and rolled oats which are grown in Sussex and have an outstanding nutty flavour and in my opinion taste far superior to the usual oats. Oat groats are the whole oats which need to be soaked and sprouted before use. Rolled oats have been flaked and can be soaked first and used for porridge and flapjacks or ground into flour for raw cakes and pastries.

■ Oils

My preferred oils are coconut, flax, hemp and olive oil. Coconut oil is a monounsaturated fat, which health experts are starting to believe is essential in the diet because of the essential fatty acids it contains, mainly lauric acid. Coconut oil is the only fat which is not metabolised by the liver, and is a superb source of energy. It is anti-microbial, anti-viral, and balances the metabolism. Flax oil is the highest dietary source of the omega 3 essential fatty acids, which is the one Western diets mostly lack. Hemp oil is the only food which is the perfect balance of omegas 3, 6, and 9. They have very different but equally delicious flavours: flax is buttery, hemp is nuttier. When buying oils, look for those in dark glass bottles – with the exception of coconut oil, which is very stable, oils are sensitive to both heat and light. If an olive oil states it is from the first cold pressing, this should guarantee that it is raw. Olive oil is a great liver cleanser.

■ Olives

Are they raw or aren't they? Sadly, the answer is probably no. We are now lucky enough to get guaranteed raw olives from the US, but they are outrageously expensive. The only raw brands I know of in the UK are made by Sunita, their green pitted olives with herbs, and the Bella di Cerignola olives which are fatter and juicier and contain stones. In the main, it is probably safer to assume your olives have been heat treated. Steer clear of olives in brine and olives in tins, which are generally pasteurised. Pitted olives, too, are more likely to have been through intensive heat.

■ Sauerkraut

Fermented cabbage usually made with sea salt and juniper berries, sauerkraut is wonderful for the digestion because of its high enzymatic activity and the friendly bacteria it contains. It is a good source of vitamin C and helps strengthen the immune system. Most sauerkraut is heat-treated; we recommend the Bionova one which is unpasteurised.

■ Seagreens

One of my very favourite ingredients, Seagreens is a UK produced wild wrack seaweed granule that has a complete nutritional profile, i.e. it contains all the vitamins and minerals the body needs. It adds texture, flavour and nutrition to just about any savoury dish you can think of. It is expensive, but you only need a little – one teaspoon per serving is ample.

■ Sea vegetables

Sea vegetables, as the most mineral rich foods found in nature, deserve to be a staple part of everybody's diet. We use dulse, a purple sea vegetable, and our firm favourite (I can eat a whole packet in one sitting), which just needs a light rinsing under the tap, and is a wonderful source of calcium. Arame is stringy, needs soaking for 20 minutes, and is also popular because of its mild taste – very good with grated vegetables. Hijiki is similar to arame, but slightly fatter, with a more intense flavour, and needs soaking for up to an hour, in which time it will treble or even quadruple in size. Wakame is green and leathery, and must be soaked for 10 minutes before adding to salads. Nori sheets are an essential item in the raw food pantry for making nori rolls, the rawfooders' sandwich. The light green sheets have been toasted so are not raw, search for dark green ones. Nori flakes and Atlantic sea salad are powdered sea veg which are perfect for using as a salad or soup garnish. Sea spaghetti is another favourite, it has an outstanding flavour, you can simply stir some into a creamy sauce for a raw tagliatelle. Then there's kelp, a powdered sea vegetable, which is an amazingly rich in minerals, especially iodine. We eat it every day; adults only need 1/2-1 teaspoon a day, so you can add it to most dishes and barely notice the fishy flavour.

Clearspring is the UK's most popular brand of sea vegetables. Clearspring dulse and wakame are raw; all the other varieties are heated at over 38°C. But I think sea vegetables are such an important part of the diet that it is better to eat them even though they have been heat-treated than not at all. We also recommend the French seaweed brand Bord a Bord which are not heat treated and preserved in sea salt. They need thorough rinsing before use but are very fresh and taste like they have come straight off the sea shore.

■ Sweeteners

People often ask me what I use as a sweetener: there is really only one good raw alternative, and that is agave nectar, which comes from a Mexican cactus plant, has a low glycaemic index, and tastes gorgeous – similar to maple syrup. Also new on the market is yacon syrup, which is made from the Peruvian yacon root, and contains only fructoligosaccharides, a sugar which is not absorbed by the body. It has a malty flavour and is good to use as a spread or topping. However, if you are unwilling to shell out for these on a daily basis, there are plenty of alternatives on the wholefood market, which may not be raw, but are relatively healthful. You can buy agave syrup, manufactured by Allos or Biona – not raw, but less than half the price. Then there's apple concentrate or date syrup, which come from natural fruit sources; molasses, rich in essential minerals; and maple syrup, the American's favourite. Any of these are acceptable if you're not strict about raw, and not having them in large amounts. Stevia is a herb which comes in powdered or liquid form. It is incredibly sweet (300 times sweeter than sugar) so you only need a tiny amount. It can be hard to get it right with stevia: too much and the taste is like strong liquorice, not enough and your dish will lack sweetness. It is illegal to sell stevia as a sweetener in the UK and the US, and most people in the health food industry believe this is down to pressure from the sugar manufacturers, rather than any proven health risks.

- Tamari, shoyu, miso, liquid aminos, hemp sauce, Himalayan crystal salt

These are seasonings that we use to add a salty element to our recipes, and bring out the flavours of a dish. They are very strong so use sparingly – the less the better. I recommend Clearspring as a good brand for tamari and shoyu; these are natural forms of soy sauce, tamari is wheat-free. Look out for miso that is unpasteurised; we use one made by Source Foods which is made from geothermic Icelandic sea salt with a low sodium content. Although miso is not a raw food, it is a living food; due to the fermentation process it contains living enzymes. The original liquid aminos is made by Braggs; far easier to find in the UK is that made by Marigold. Paul Bragg was a raw food pioneer in the USA, and this product used to be very popular, but there is some controversy over it now because it contains hydrolyzed vegetable protein, and has naturally occurring MSG. My personal view is that a heavily processed product like this is never going to be good if you consume it by the tablespoon, but a dash on a salad will liven it up without causing the body any undue harm. Hemp sauce has a similar taste to liquid aminos, and is made with fermented hemp seeds and sea salt. It makes a good stock substitute in sauces and gravies. Himalayan crystal salt is an amazing pink salt found in one of the purest places on earth. Rich in minerals, it also aids absorption, and I love to add a pinch to savoury or sweet dishes. You can also use crystal sea salt if you prefer.

- Vanilla

Pods are the freshest and most flavoursome option for whizzing up in your creams, ice creams and sweets. If you are not using your blender, you can slit open the pod with a knife and scrape out the seeds to add to your recipe. Vanilla pods must be stored in an airtight container to preserve their taste and aroma. If you haven't got vanilla pods, vanilla extract is the next best option. This is not raw, and is preserved in alcohol, but it is pure vanilla. Steer clear of vanilla essence which is a pale imitation of the real thing.

■ Vegetables

Where the recipe states '2 carrots' or '1 onion', this is taken to mean one average-sized vegetable. Please don't be afraid to play around with the amounts, and adjust them accordingly. For instance if your carrots are very large, and the recipe calls for two, perhaps it is better to just use one and a half; conversely, if your onions are very small, and the recipe asks for a half, better to use a whole one. One of the beauties of raw food preparation is that it is very hard to go wrong – it is not like traditional cookery where if your eggs are not whisked enough or your sauce not hot enough, disastrous results may befall you. Rather, be intuitive with your recipes, and the dish will taste wonderfully different every time.

Try and buy seasonally and locally wherever you can; it's best not to go chasing after ingredients that have been flown half way across the world, especially when home grown produce tastes so much better. Organic is preferable but not always the best option; I would argue that when it comes to flavour and nutrition, it's better to buy an English apple that is not certified organic than an organic one from New Zealand. If the vegetable or fruit you are after is not in season in Europe, see if you can source an alternative that is. When buying salad greens look for minimal packaging; not only is all that plastic bad for the environment it is affecting the quality of the produce too.

■ Vinegar

A good quality, unpasteurised apple cider vinegar, such as that made by Aspall's, should be raw. We also occasionally use rice vinegar and balsamic vinegar, which are not raw. Other alternatives include lemon juice and lime juice.

■ Dips

Why so many dips? They really are a staple of the raw food diet, like the sandwich is to a conventional diet. Endlessly versatile, they turn a humble carrot into a feast. We usually have dips every day, either for lunch or tea. A recipe can be simply tweaked to create a whole new taste experience; the same dip can be used in different ways to create an amazing variety of dishes.

Our favourite vegetables for dipping are carrot sticks, broccoli florets, baby sweetcorn, sugar snaps, and sweet potato (peel and cut into sticks like carrot). But really, you can use anything – mushrooms, cauliflower, pepper, celery, cucumber, anything at all. Serve a selection with one or two dips and maybe some crisps made in the dehydrator and you have a quick and delicious light meal or snack. Dips are perfect for parties, easy to do when you're catering for large numbers of people, and very attractive, if you fan the different coloured veg out in a serving dish.

Another raw staple is to make roll-ups with nori sheets. Spread the dip on the sheet, sprinkle with a few sprouts and some finely chopped veg, and roll up (see *Eat Smart Eat Raw* for more roll-up suggestions). You can try them with lettuce leaves, cabbage, or Chinese leaf too.

You can also add a little water, thin them out, and make rich and interesting dressings for salads. Just mix some green leaf in a bowl, and hey presto! A gourmet dinner in minutes.

You're also allowed to eat them with a packet of crisps or tortilla chips. Then you can indulge your cravings and get some super-nutrition in you at the same time.

Another tip: dehydrate leftovers. Spread thinly on a sheet and when they're dry store in an airtight tub in the fridge. Then crumble onto a salad for a bit of texture. Dehydrating intensifies the flavours to create delicious raw 'croûtons'.

- 10 mins and soaking 4-8hrs
- Blender
- **Serves four to six**

Hemp Seed Hummus

This was our favourite dip for a long time. One tablespoon of sesame seeds contains eight times as much calcium as a cup of cow's milk, so it's great for growing children, and the hemp seeds ensure they get a good dose of those essential fatty acids. It's full of protein, but not too dense.

- 200 g/7 oz sesame seeds, soaked 4-8 hrs
- 60 g/2 oz hemp seeds, soaked 4-8 hrs
- 1 lemon, juiced
- 1 tbsp olive oil
- 1 clove garlic
- 1/2 tsp Himalayan crystal salt
- 250 ml/8 fl oz water

Drain the sesame seeds and hemp seeds. Put everything in the blender together, and blend to make a creamy paste. The sesame seeds will break down completely, although you'll be left with black specks in the mixture from the hemp seeds, which crack open and release their beautiful rich oils. Keep in the fridge and eat within five days.

■ ■ ■ ■ Did you know that George Washington was a hemp farmer, and the US declaration of Independence was written on hemp paper?

- 5 mins
- Blender
- **Serves four**

Reuben's Guacamole Dip

My boys have always been fussy about avocados. Getting one that is a little overripe puts them off eating them. They insisted that they wouldn't eat guacamole, but I adore it. So I took their favourite dip (Reuben's dip from *Eat Smart Eat Raw*) combined the two and created something we all love.

- 1 tbsp apple cider vinegar
- 1 large avocado
- 1 large tomato
- 2 tbsp tahini
- 1 tsp miso
- 1 tbsp nutritional yeast flakes
- 1 tsp kelp powder

Juice the lemon, add the juice to the blender. Peel and pit the avocado, and add the flesh to the blender. Quarter the tomato, and add it into the blender with all the remaining ingredients. Blend to a cream. Serve with crudités. For a quick snack, spread some on a romaine lettuce leaf, add some alfalfa, roll up and munch.

■ ■ ■ ■ If you're into superfoods, sprinkle some raw cacao nibs or bee pollen into your guacamole for an extra buzz.

- 10 mins
- Blender
- **Serves four**

Red Pepper Ketchup

Wow! Much better than the tomato version, and healthier too.
Red peppers have a really high water content: if you blend them up,
they turn surprisingly liquid. Alternatively, use yellow peppers for a
golden ketchup.

- 60 g/2 oz dried tomatoes
- 3 red peppers
- 4 dates
- 1/2 onion
- 1 tbsp apple cider vinegar

If you're using shop-bought dried tomatoes, you will need to soak
them for up to an hour to soften them a bit first. Remove the stem and
seeds, and chop the red peppers as small as you need to for your
blender, then pop them in. Pit the dates, peel the onion, and add them
in with the vinegar and tomatoes. Blend the whole lot together.
The resulting blend should be the same consistency as ketchup –
dollopy. Good with burgers, or just as a dip with crudités.

■ ■ ■ ■ Tomatoes are highly acidic, and avoided both by followers of
macrobiotics, and Hippocrates practitioners.

- 10 mins
- Blender
- **Serves four**

■ Carrot Ketchup

Another alternative to tomato ketchup, carrots have a lovely fruity flavour when puréed into a dip.

- 60 g/2 oz dried tomatoes
- 4 carrots
- 4 dates, pitted
- 1/2 onion, peeled and chopped
- 1 tbsp apple cider vinegar
- 1 tsp miso
- 1 tsp kelp
- 125 ml/4 fl oz water

If you're using shop-bought sun-dried tomatoes, soak them for up to an hour first. Top and tail the carrots, and cut them into small enough pieces for your blender to be happy with them. Put all the ingredients in the blender and whiz up. If your carrots are big, you may need some more water, but not too much: you want it to have the thick consistency of traditional ketchup. Serve with burgers or spread on crackers.

■ ■ ■ ■ Carrots are the richest vegetable source of vitamin A, the antioxidant which promotes good vision, hence the old wives tale that carrots make you see in the dark.

- Blender
- 5 mins
- **Serves four**

Asian Dipping Sauce

This is like those red sauces you get with your Chinese or Thai spring rolls. It's quite runny, and wouldn't really work as a dip for crudités. But it's good with spring rolls from *Eat Smart Eat Raw*, or the tempura (p 130). And it makes a super dressing on a salad of green leaves and sea vegetables.

- 3 tomatoes
- 1 red chilli, seeded
- 1 clove garlic
- 1 tbsp tamari
- 1 tbsp agave nectar
- 1 tbsp sesame oil

Cut the tomatoes into quarters. Put everything in the blender and whiz until the tomatoes are fully puréed. Keep for an hour or two before serving, and it will thicken slightly.

■ ■ ■ ■ It is a substance called capsaicin which gives chillies their heat: the more capsaicin the pepper contains, the hotter it is. Scotch bonnets and habaneros are the hottest varieties – we usually use the long thin peppers commonly found in supermarkets.

- Blender
- 5 mins
- **Serves two**

Sweet Almond Dip

This is a favourite with kids: serve with veggies like carrot, cucumber and broccoli and with any luck they will eat lots. Also makes a lovely dressing thinned with a little water.

- 1 tbsp agave nectar
- 2 tbsp almond butter
- 1 tbsp flax oil
- 1 tbsp nutritional yeast flakes

Put them all in a bowl and give them a good mix together with a spoon.

■ ■ ■ ■ Almonds are rich in monounsaturated fats, which have been associated with reduced risk of heart disease, and have been shown to lower cholesterol.

- ■ 10 mins and presoaking 4-8 hrs
- ■ Blender
- ■ **Serves four**

■ Parsley Dip

Lemons always add a tangy edge to any dip, and here they bring the flavours of the parsley to life. This is a very adult dip, children tend to find the parsley too overpowering, but it works in just about any way you choose to serve it – as a spread, a dip, in roll-ups, or as a dressing.

- ■ 1 large bunch parsley
- ■ 90 g/3 oz sesame seeds, soaked 4-8 hrs
- ■ 4 tbsp olive oil
- ■ 2 lemons, juiced
- ■ 1 tsp kelp
- ■ 2 cloves garlic

Prepare the parsley, chopping it down so it will fit nicely in your blender. Drain the sesame seeds. Put everything in the blender and purée until smooth. If you don't have a high speed blender, you may find this hard work. Chop the parsley really fine, and consider substituting half or all the sesame seeds for tahini.

■ ■ ■ ■ There are two varieties of parsley most commonly found in the UK, flat leaf and curly. Curly has a more intense flavour, and the flat leaf is more fragrant. We like to use both, depending how the mood takes us.

- 10 mins
- Blender
- **Serves four**

Zachary's Dip

When I was weaning my youngest son, this was his (and my) favourite lunch. Once he'd got past the baby food stage, I carried on making it as a dip. It's sweet without being too sugary, a lovely light dip, and with all that broccoli, very nutritious.

- 2 pears
- 2 small heads broccoli
- 1 tbsp flax seed oil
- 2 tbsp tahini
- 2 tbsp nori flakes

Chop the pears and remove the cores and stems. Put them in the blender and they will easily turn to pulp. Add the broccoli, oil, and tahini, and blend again. Check no broccoli heads have escaped the blades, and are hiding in the purée. Stir in the nori flakes by hand, or blend briefly. When you're sure it's all blended together, serve in lettuce wraps or nori rolls with lots of alfalfa.

■ ■ ■ ■ Pears are a good source of the trace mineral copper – an average pear contains 10% of the RDA.

- 5 mins, soaking 4-8 hrs
- Blender
- **Serves four; makes one jar**

Coriander Chutney

Adapted from an authentic Indian recipe, this goes well with the onion bhajis from *Eat Smart Eat Raw*. It's a creamy, pungent chutney, quite complex in flavour and slightly spicy. It's also lovely in lettuce wraps teamed up with a heap of beansprouts.

- 1 large bunch coriander
- ½ onion
- 1 chilli, stem and seeds removed
- 1 lime, juiced
- 1 tsp garam masala
- 2 dates, pitted
- 1 tsp tamari
- 2 tbsp almonds, soaked 4-8 hrs
- 125 ml/4 fl oz water

Loosely chop the coriander. Put everything in the blender together and blend to a thick purée.

■ ■ ■ ■ Along with basil and parsley, coriander is a staple in our kitchen. We often add a few sprigs to our vegetable juice, or snip a few leaves into a salad to add an exquisite something extra.

- 5 mins
- Blender
- **Serves four**

■ Date Chutney

Gorgeous with burgers instead of ketchup.

- 150 g/5 oz fresh dates, pitted
- 2 tbsp apple cider vinegar
- 1 tbsp sesame oil
- 1/2 cm/1/4 in piece root ginger
- 1 clove garlic
- 1/2 red chilli

Put everything in the blender, it should turn to a cream more or less instantly if you're using good soft dates. Just make sure there are no pieces of garlic or chilli left unprocessed!

■ ■ ■ ■ Chilli peppers have amazing healing properties. They are said to fight inflammation, reduce congestion, and boost immunity, even reduce the risk of cardio-vascular disease.

- 5 mins
- Blender
- **Serves four**

Lemon Pickle

Carley's are an organic producer based in Cornwall, who make superior quality gourmet foods. They do a selection of raw nut butters that are very popular (pecan, rainforest, and mixed seed); they also make these fabulous preserved raw lemons. They go great in salads, but I love to eat them in this addictive chutney. Beware though, they are quite salty, so don't overdo it.

- 1 red chilli
- 4 fresh dates, pitted
- 1 cm/$1/2$ root ginger
- 1 clove garlic
- 2 tbsp olive oil
- 200 g/7 oz preserved lemons

Remove and discard the stem and seeds of the chilli. Put everything except the lemons in the blender, and blend to a purée, being careful to make sure there are no bits of chilli or garlic left. If you're using a high power blender, you can put the lemons in, and blend them on a slow setting (a 3 or a 4) to make sure they stay chunky. If not, you can process them in the food processor, or chop them by hand, and then stir them back in. You want them in chunks roughly the size of hazelnuts. Store in the fridge – it keeps well. It goes great with burgers, as a dip for crisps, or as a piquant salad dressing.

■ ■ ■ ■ In the US in the mid 19th century, lemons were highly prized for their ability to protect against scurvy, so much so that they were sold for as much as $1 each!

■ Pâtés and spreads

Pâtés are always a winner stuffed in a pepper: just half
the pepper lengthways, de-seed it and fill it with pâté.
Cucumbers are good sliced crossways and spread with pâté
to make little canapés. They're also easy to do spread on a
lettuce leaf or nori sheet and rolled. Some of them are stiff
enough that you can roll them into balls and serve them as
little falafel-y things with a sauce. If you have a dehydrator,
even better, pop the balls in for a few hours to make them
crunchy and draw out the flavours. And of course, you can
just use them as spreads for crackers and breads.

- ■ 5 mins, soaking one hour
- ■ Blender
- ■ **Makes one small jar**

■ Tapenade

Tapenade is a Mediterranean olive spread best made with pitted olives. Basically it's just an excuse to eat lots of olives, which are one of the best sources of healthy fats and protein around. This is a wonderfully rich earthy dip, best spread sparingly on bread or crackers, or it makes a marvellous dressing on a pile of green leaves and sprouts.

- ■ 90 g/3 oz olives, pitted
- ■ 30 g/1 oz dried tomatoes
- ■ 1 tbsp olive oil
- ■ 1 tsp vinegar
- ■ 1 clove garlic, crushed

If you are using shop-bought dried tomatoes, you will need to soak them for up to an hour first. Unless you have a high powered blender, you may find your food processor works better for this recipe. Just pop all the ingredients in, and blitz until completely puréed, with no bits of tomato left visible.

■ ■ ■ ■ There is an olive tree in Croatia which has been determined by tree ring analysis to be nearly two thousand years old, and is still producing fruit. I would love to try some of those olives!

- ■ Blender
- ■ 10 mins
- ■ **Serves four**

■ Olive Pâté

This is like a less rich version of Tapenade, so you can be more liberal with it. Try it on crackers or in roll-ups.

- ■ 2 tomatoes
- ■ 1 stick celery
- ■ 1 sprig parsley
- ■ 90 g/3 oz olives
- ■ 1/2 red chilli, seeded
- ■ 2 tbsp dulse
- ■ 1 tbsp olive oil

Quarter the tomatoes, and chop the celery and parsley down a little. Put everything in the blender and process until smooth.

■ ■ ■ ■ Olives are one of the best dietary sources of vitamin E, the fat soluble antioxidant. They are also rich in monounsaturated fats, and it is this combination that makes them exceptional nutritionally.

- Blender
- 5 mins, presoaking 8-12 hrs
- **Serves four**

Cashew Cream Cheese

This is lush, a good one to serve to non-raw fooders, it's so irresistible. If you're feeling extravagant, you can make it with macadamias or pine nuts for a real gourmet treat.

- 120 g/4 oz cashews, presoaked 8-12 hrs
- 1 lemon, juiced
- 1 tsp miso
- 1/2 onion
- 250 ml/8 fl oz water
- 1 bunch chives

Put all your ingredients, apart from the chives, in the blender and keep it on for a good few minutes. Snip the chives into tiny pieces, as small as you can, with scissors, and then stir them in by hand. Cashews have a habit of hiding in the mix as little chunks unless you blend really thoroughly. If you store it in a jar in the fridge, it will thicken further.

■ ■ ■ ■ Cashews are generally heat-treated because the inside of the shell contains a caustic resin used to make insecticides. They are steamed at high temperatures to remove the nut from the shell without the resin. You can buy really raw cashews from online raw food stores.

- 5 mins, presoaking 8-12 hrs
- Blender
- **Serves eight; makes two jars**

■ Happy Pâté

This is one of my favourites. It's a really vibrant, fruity combination, especially popular with children due to its natural sweetness.

- ½ red pepper
- 2 carrots
- 1 tomato
- 60 g/2 oz almonds, presoaked 8-12 hrs
- 2 dates, pitted
- 1 lemon, juiced

Prepare the pepper, carrots and tomatoes and chop so they'll fit in your blender. Add the remaining ingredients and blend. If it's too much for your blender, add a little water or olive oil to help it along. Serve with green crudités such as broccoli, cucumber and celery for a quick and easy snack lunch. Store in the fridge, and eat within a few days.

■ ■ ■ ■ Almonds are actually seeds, which come from the fruit of the almond tree. They are from the same family of trees as apricots and peaches. I don't know why we never eat almond fruit!

- 5 mins, presoaking 8-12 hrs
- Blender
- **Serves eight; makes two jars**

■ Sunshine Pâté

This is based on the Sunshine Soup from *Eat Smart Eat Raw*. It's like a more adult version of the previous recipe; a little spicier and denser. It's a bit too thick to use as a dip, but good for spreading in nori rolls or lettuce leaves.

- 2 carrots
- 2 tomatoes
- 1 yellow pepper
- 120 g/4 oz almonds, presoaked 8-12 hrs
- 1 tsp tamari
- 1 lemon, juiced
- 1 tsp cumin powder

Prepare your carrots, tomatoes and peppers by removing unwanted bits and chopping them small enough to fit into your blender easily. Pop them in (tip – put the tomatoes in the bottom because they liquidise easier and are not so likely to get stuck in the blades), and blend until smooth. Then add in the remaining ingredients, and keep blending until there are no lumps of nut left. Store in the fridge – it will only keep for a few days.

■ ■ ■ ■ We always make sure to remove all the seeds from our peppers. Although they are edible, they are bitter, and contain no particular nutritional benefits.

- 10 mins, 8-12 hrs soaking
- Blender
- **Serves four to six**

Walnut Pâté

A lovely dense, meaty pâté that makes a good stuffing for peppers or nori rolls.

- 2 sticks celery
- 1 red pepper
- 300 g/10 oz walnuts, soaked 8-12 hrs
- 1 lemon, juiced
- 1 tbsp white miso
- 60 g/2 oz dried tomatoes
- 4 tbsp water

Chop the celery, remove the stem and seeds of the pepper, and chop. Put everything in the blender and blend to a cream.

■ ■ ■ ■ Most people know by now that fish and flax seeds are a good source of the valuable omega- 3 fatty acids, but did you know that walnuts are also a great way to get these fats in your diet? 25 g walnuts contain about 90% of the RDA.

- 5 mins, soaking 8-12 hrs
- Blender
- **Serves four, 500 ml, one large jar**

Hazelnut and Apple Pâté

This is a gorgeous, light, creamy pâté, good in nori rolls.

- 1 apple
- 1 tomato
- 1 stick celery
- 120 g/4 oz hazelnuts, soaked 8-12 hrs
- 1 tbsp dried tomatoes
- 1 tsp white miso
- 2 tbsp olive oil
- 2 tbsp apple cider vinegar

Prepare the apple, tomato and celery for your blender. Put everything in and blend to a thick purée.

■ ■ ■ ■ Adding a little apple to any savoury dish is a great way to lighten it up and create a contrast of flavours. Sprinkle grated apple into a salad, or blend half an apple into a soup or sauce.

- 5 mins, 4-8 hrs soaking
- Blender
- **Makes one large jar**

■ Pine Nut Pâté

This is very versatile – it makes a yummy dip or a rich dressing, it's great in roll-ups, or dehydrate it for a very tasty salad garnish.

- 120 g/4 oz pine nuts, soaked 4-8 hrs
- 1 tbsp olive oil
- 1 small bunch basil
- 3 tomatoes, chopped
- 1 clove garlic
- 2 tsp white miso

Put everything in the blender. You shouldn't need any liquid, the tomatoes will be enough. Blend for a few minutes until you have a light green cream.

■ ■ ■ ■ Pine nuts may be expensive, but they are very popular in raw food cuisine for the creamy richness they impart to a dish, and their exquisite fragrant taste. We buy ours in bulk and store them in an airtight container in the dark so they keep well.

■ Dressings

Dressings can transform a simple salad into something amazing. Take a plateful of fresh leaves like rocket or corn salad: add a spicy dressing to wake you up; a creamy dressing to soothe you; a fruity dressing to cheer you; a green dressing for cleansing; or an acidic dressing for a bit of zing. The resulting salad will be wildly different every time – who said raw food was boring? There's one here to suit your every mood.

My favourite, simple dressing is flax oil, apple cider vinegar, Seagreens, and nutritional yeast flakes.

- Blender or food processor
- 10 mins
- **Serves four**

Pesto

I finally started making my own pesto, and it was a revelation.
You need a large bunch of basil (if you're buying it in the supermarket, you may need two or three times what they consider a bunch), so it's not cheap. But the taste of pesto made with fresh basil is incomparable to the stuff that comes out of a jar. It's too rich to really use as a dip, but you could spread it on bread. Best as a dressing for salad.

- 1 large bunch basil, loosely chopped
- 60 g/2 oz pine nuts
- 2 tbsp nutritional yeast flakes
- 2 tbsp olive oil
- 1 tbsp agave nectar
- 1 tsp apple cider vinegar
- 2 cloves garlic
- 1 tsp tamari

Using your blender or your food processor put everything in and keep going until the basil is completely broken down and you have a thick gorgeous green goo.

■ ■ ■ ■ Make some courgetti in your spiral slicer and cover it in this, and hey pesto! You've got yourself a simply lovely dinner (see p 144).

- 5 mins
- Blender
- **Serves four**

Avo Pesto

So quick, so easy, so yummy!

- 1 avocado
- 1 bunch basil
- 2 tbsp olive oil
- 2 lemons, juiced
- 2 cloves garlic
- 2 dates
- 1 tsp miso

Stone the avocado, scoop out the flesh, and put it in the blender.
Cut the stems off the basil, chop loosely, and add to the blender with
all the other ingredients. This is great on any salad, especially as a sort
of coleslaw with grated veg like carrots and cabbage.

■ ■ ■ ■ Adding avocado to salads can help with the absorption of
both the anti-oxidants lycopene (found in tomatoes) and
carotene (found in carrots). It is the monounsaturated fats in
avocado which enhance the bioavailability of these nutrients.
Which goes part way to explaining why rawfooders have a
tendency to put avocado in everything!

- 10 mins
- Blender
- **Serves four**

Coriander Pesto

Hands up those who thought you could only make pesto with basil? OK, technically you are probably correct, but this version using fresh coriander instead is just as delicious.

- 1 bunch coriander
- 1 chilli
- 4 tbsp olive oil
- 75 g/2$\frac{1}{2}$ oz Brazil nuts
- 2 limes, juiced
- 2 cloves garlic
- 2 dates
- 1 tsp tamari

Loosely chop the coriander. Prepare the chilli, remove the seeds and stem. Put everything in the blender and keep going until you have a thick cream. If you're blender does not have a very strong motor, you may need to add a little water to help it turn.

■ ■ ■ ■ Brazil nuts are one of the easiest nuts to make raw nut butter with. Put them in your blender or food processor and keep it on for a few minutes until it starts to get hot. If they're not runny already, leave the mixture to cool down for five minutes and repeat the process. Store fresh nut butters in the fridge to stop them going rancid.

- 10 mins
- Blender
- **Serves two**

Coconut Satay

Fresh coconut is an incredible food, full of healthy fats like lauric acid, an essential fatty acid found also in mothers' breast milk. It combines well with dates, and this dressing manages to be both refreshing and substantial.

- 120 g/4 oz coconut meat
- 2 tbsp olive oil
- 4 dates, pitted
- 1/2 chilli, deseeded
- 1 lemon, juiced
- 125 ml/4 fl oz water

Remove the flesh from the coconut shell. This involves a trick with a hammer and a chisel that I'm not very good at. Prise the flesh out of the nut with the chisel. Chop the coconut meat into small pieces and put in the blender with the other ingredients. If you have a high power blender, it will go gorgeously creamy. In a standard blender, the coconut won't break down completely, but you will still get a lovely mixture which works great as a dressing over some fresh green leaves. Eat within a day or two as fresh coconut goes rancid quickly.

■ ■ ■ ■ To extract coconut flesh, find somewhere to place the coconut securely against, a doorstep is ideal. Whack the top with the hammer about a third of the way down, rotate it slightly and whack it again, and rotate and whack it again. Once you've whacked it three times, the top should be easily prised off. Pour out the water and drink it, it's wonderful.

- Blender
- 5 mins, presoaking 12 hrs
- **Serves four to six**

■ Walnut Dressing

This is a very tasty, tangy dip to liven up your salad when you've only got a few things left in the fridge, and are feeling devoid of inspiration. Goes well on grated vegetables or a heap of leaves.

- 150 g/5 oz walnuts, presoaked 8-12 hrs
- 1 lemon, juiced
- 1/2 onion
- 1 tsp tamari
- 60 g/2 oz dried tomatoes
- 250 ml/8 fl oz water

Chuck everything in the blender and whiz away. If you have a dehydrator, dry the leftover. It makes a gorgeous garnish, crumbled into a salad.

■ ■ ■ ■ Walnuts are good 'brain food'! Not just because they look like little brains, but because they are an excellent source of omega 3 fatty acids which promote mental clarity and focus.

- 10 mins, sprouting
- Blender
- **Serves four to six**

Creamy Cucumber Dressing

A creamy but surprisingly light dressing and all that cucumber makes it very alkalising.

- 1 cucumber
- 120 g/4 oz sprouted sunflower seeds (p 42)
- 2 cloves garlic
- 1 lemon, juiced
- 1 tsp white miso

Chop the cucumber into pieces small enough for your blender to handle. Blend everything up – it should whiz away quite easily. Pour over a pile of green leaves. This is so good; you could even eat it as a soup.

■ ■ ■ ■ Sunflower seeds are one of the easiest seeds to sprout, a great one to start with. They only take a day or two before they are at their best – don't leave them too long or they will go brown.

- Blender
- 5 mins
- **Serves four; makes one small jar**

■ Sweet Chilli Sauce

You can buy a cooked version of this in Asian grocers and supermarkets, it's basically sugar and spice. The sweet taste makes the heat more palatable. It's traditionally used as a dipping sauce for spring rolls and barbecues, but we use it as a salad dressing.

- 16 dates, pitted
- 2 red chillies, seeded
- 3 cloves garlic
- 1 cm/$^{1}/_{2}$ in piece root ginger
- 2 limes, juiced
- 2 tbsp water

Prepare all your ingredients, and then put them in the blender with the water. Add more water if you want a runnier dressing: I like it nice and thick so it coats the salad well.

■ ■ ■ Ginger is very good for the digestion, soothing and calming to the intestines, which is why it is a popular home remedy for morning sickness during pregnancy.

- 5 mins, 10-20 mins soaking
- Blender
- **Serves four**

Pineapple Dressing

This is a sharp, vibrant dressing. Take a plateful of rocket, mix in some avocado and beansprouts, toss it in this dressing, and you have a meal fit for a king.

- 60 g/2 oz dried pineapple, soaked 10–20 mins
- 1/2 cm/1/4 in piece root ginger
- 1 clove garlic
- 1 lemon, juiced
- 2 tbsp sesame oil
- 2 tbsp water

Soak the pineapple in advance. When it is ready, drain it and add it to the blender with all the other ingredients. Blend everything for a minute or two, making sure there are no bits of ginger left floating.

■ ■ ■ ■ Variations: replace the dried pineapple with dried papaya or dried mango. Tropical Wholefoods manufacture high quality sun-dried fruits.

- 5 mins
- Blender
- Serves four

■ Red Pepper Dressing

Red peppers and lemons are just such a great combination. Together they produce an unbelievably tangy fruitiness. This dressing takes literally seconds to make, and yet can transform a simple plate of leaves. Try it drizzled on rocket.

- 1 red pepper
- 2 tbsp olive oil
- 1 lemon, juiced
- 1 clove garlic
- 1 tbsp herbs de Provence

Remove the stem and seeds from the pepper. Chop it coarsely, and pop in the blender. Add the olive oil, lemon juice and garlic and blend to a liquid. Stir in the herbs by hand, and serve immediately.

■ ■ ■ ■ Herbs de Provence is an aromatic mix of dried herbs, usually containing thyme, basil, marjoram, bay leaf and rosemary.

■ Soups

Soups are about the easiest thing to make. All you need
is a good blender, and you can have a great meal ready in
minutes. Serve with some Essene bread or crackers and
you've got a feast. Most raw soups don't really suit heating,
but you can just gently warm them if you want something
hot, especially in the winter. We use a porringer, which is a
double saucepan that heats the water in the bottom pan,
and so provides a more gentle heat for the top pan. Or you
can put your soup in a Pyrex bowl in a saucepan of nearly
boiling water. All the soups benefit from a sprinkling of dulse
flakes (Atlantic sea salad), nori flakes or nutritional yeast
flakes and some alfalfa artfully strewn across the top.

- 5 mins
- Blender
- **Serves two**

■ Chick Pea Soup

Creamy like hummus, this is a very filling soup. Don't over sprout chick peas – the tails shouldn't be any longer than the beans or they start to taste a bit woody.

- 300 g/10 oz chick peas, sprouted
- 250 ml/8 fl oz carrot juice
- 3 tomatoes, chopped
- 1 tbsp tamari
- 4 tbsp olive oil
- 2 tbsp dulse, rinsed
- 2 tbsp dried tomatoes
- 2 cloves garlic
- 1/2 red chilli
- 500 ml/16 fl oz water
- 1 tbsp nori flakes

Chop the tomatoes. Chuck everything (except the nori flakes) in a blender and whiz until there's no point whizzing anymore – should take a couple of minutes. Pour into bowls and garnish with the nori.

■ ■ ■ ■ Chick peas are exceptionally nutritious, being an excellent source of protein and trace minerals, especially molybdenum and manganese.

- 5 mins
- Blender
- **Serves one**

Fantastic Fennel Soup

Fennel is one of my favourite vegetables, and makes a wonderfully light, simple and refreshing soup. My other favourite fennel recipe is on p 109. I also juice it a lot; it's a lovely addition to a green juice.

- 6 tomatoes
- 1 avocado
- 1 head fennel
- 1 clove garlic
- 1 tbsp olive oil
- 1 tbsp tamari
- Handful alfalfa sprouts

Prepare all the vegetables for the blender. Put the tomatoes in first because they are so liquid, they will be easier for the blades to start with. Reserve the alfalfa sprouts, and put everything else in the blender. Whiz for a minute, then pour into bowls and serve. Garnish with alfalfa sprouts.

■ ■ ■ ■ Fennel also makes excellent chewing gum! Chew on a stalk for extra fresh breath.

- 10 mins
- Blender
- **Serves two**

■ Beetroot Soup

This is my favourite all time soup. Sweet and spicy (if you're making it for children, just omit the chilli). If you're family aren't keen on beetroot, try them with this, they might be surprised.

- 2 beetroots
- 1 carrot
- 3 tomatoes
- 1 red chilli
- 2 dates
- 2 tbsp olive oil
- 1 tsp tamari
- 250 ml/8 fl oz water
- 1 tbsp dulse flakes
- 1 tsp nutritional yeast flakes
- 1 tbsp pine nuts

Top, tail and peel the beetroot. Chop into blender-friendly pieces. Top, tail and chop the carrot, and cut the tomatoes into quarters. Seed the red chilli, pit the dates. Put all your prepared veg in the blender, along with the olive oil and tamari (tomatoes at the bottom to make it easy for your blender). Blend for a couple of minutes until you're satisfied there's no lumpy bits left. Pour into bowls and sprinkle with dulse, nutritional yeast, and pine nuts.

■ ■ ■ ■ There is nothing quite like beetroot. Betacyanin is the pigment which stains your hands, chopping boards and nice white tops...but hey it's also a powerful antioxidant, so that's ok.

- 5 mins, presoaking 8-12 hrs
- Blender
- **Serves one**

Sweetcorn and Almond Soup

We try and eat seasonally in the main. This means that foods like sweetcorn, which have a short season from July to September become treats, delights which we anticipate all year round. In the sweetcorn season, we eat it two or three times a week; it's great raw, straight off the cob. Then it's over, and we wait for next year's crop. Like mince pies or crème eggs, eating seasonally is fun.

- 1 cob sweetcorn (approx 120 g/4 oz)
- 1 stick celery
- 1/2 onion
- 30 g/1 oz almonds, soaked overnight
- 250 ml/8 fl oz water
- 1 tsp brown miso
- 1 tbsp olive oil
- 1/2 tbsp nori flakes

Strip the corn of its outer leaves, and remove the kernels from the cob by standing it over a bowl and slicing carefully downwards with your knife, positioning the blade between the kernels and the cob. Roughly chop the celery and onion, and put them in the blender with the corn and the remaining ingredients (reserve the nori flakes). Blend for a good few minutes, making sure there are no bits of corn or almond left. Pour into bowls and sprinkle with nori flakes as garnish.

■ ■ ■ Corn comes in many colours, not just yellow, but blue, red, pink, black and even purple. Purple corn is a rare and powerful antioxidant which is becoming a popular superfood.

- 10 mins and presoaking 8-12 hrs
- Blender
- **Serves two**

Autumn Leaves Soup

Reuben named this because of the colours, and the dulse garnish looks like leaves. But it's doubly appropriate because it's made with all the lovely root vegetables which start coming into season in the autumn. Use either parsnip or squash or sweet potato: they have quite distinctive flavours, and you will end up with a different soup every time.

- 500 g/1 lb root vegetables, e.g. butternut squash, sweet potato
- 2 large carrots
- 4 tomatoes
- 1/2 onion
- 2 tbsp almonds, soaked 8-12 hrs
- 1 tbsp sesame oil
- 1 tbsp agave syrup
- 1 tbsp brown rice vinegar
- 1 tbsp tamari
- 1 tbsp Chinese 5 spice
- 2 tbsp dulse flakes

Prepare your vegetables so they'll fit happily in your blender. Squash and sweet potato need peeling. Put the tomatoes in the blender first because they liquify easily and will help everything else to turn over. Put everything in but the dulse flakes. Blend up to a purée; you need a high powered blender to get a really good, creamy result. Pour into bowls and sprinkle with dulse flakes as garnish.

■ ■ ■ ■ Five spice powder is a great staple to have in your cupboard to add to dips and salad dressings. So called, because it represents each of the five elements of Chinese medicine, and encompasses all of the five flavours – salty, sour, sweet, bitter and pungent.

- 15 mins
- Blender
- **Serves two**

■ Thai Pumpkin Soup

It's worth hunting down fresh herbs and spices from an Asian grocer or well-stocked supermarket. You can buy more than you need, and freeze the extra until next time you are making a Thai recipe. Failing that, powdered versions are acceptable, or you may want to just use a ready-made Thai curry paste.

- 1 medium-sized pumpkin
- 120 g/4 oz fresh coconut meat
- 2 sticks celery
- 1 cm/$1/2$ in piece root ginger
- 1 clove garlic
- $1/2$ onion
- 1 red chilli
- 2 dates
- 1 stick lemongrass
- 2 cm/1 in piece galangal
- 1 tbsp rice vinegar
- 1 tbsp tamari
- 2 tbsp sesame oil

Scoop the flesh out of the pumpkin. There's no easy way to do this, but if you can get hold of a pumpkin scraper, they help. Put it in the blender. Prepare all the other ingredients for your blender, and pop them all in. Whiz up for a few minutes, to make a smooth, creamy soup.

■ ■ ■ ■ This is the perfect use for the pumpkin meat that is discarded from making Halloween lanterns.

- 15 mins
- Blender
- **Serves two**

Parsnip Soup

This is gorgeously sweet and creamy, perfect for a winter's lunch.

- 2 parsnips
- 2 sticks celery
- 2 small carrots
- 1 avocado
- 2 dates, pitted
- 2 cloves garlic
- 1 tbsp rice vinegar
- 1 tsp miso
- 2 tbsp flax seed oil
- 1 tbsp lecithin granules
- 600 ml/ 20 fl oz water

Prepare the veg to fit the blender. Top and tail the parsnips, and chop finely or they'll be hard to break down. Chop the celery and carrots. Halve the avocado, remove the stone and cube the flesh. Put everything in the jug and blend to a thick purée.

■ ■ ■ ■ Lecithin is derived from non GM soya, and comes in granular form. It is rich in phosphatidyl-choline which is important for brain development, and assists the body to absorb fats efficiently.

■ Salads

I first was motivated to write my first book, *Eat Smart Eat Raw* because so many people assumed to be a raw foodist meant living on lettuce and bananas. 'What do you actually eat?' was the most frequently asked question, and people couldn't believe it when I talked about Thai, burgers, noodles, and wraps. So here are even more super salad recipes, with barely a lettuce leaf in sight. While I was collecting the recipes for this book, I had been raw for about ten years and I was being pushed to find ever more inventive and creative ways of making original and interesting dinners. I explored new ingredients, and found simple and delicious ways to put them together. With two children, and another on the way, I wanted to make meals that would leave me and the family feeling full and nourished, but I didn't have the time or energy to spend long hours in the kitchen slaving over a dehydrator! Most of them are suitable either to be served individually as a meal in themselves, or if you want to liven things up a little, you can serve two smaller portions of complementary salad recipes together, or mix them with some of the recipes from the savouries section. Have a look at the sample menus chapter if you need more ideas.

- 10 mins
- Food processor
- **Serves two**

■ 'Chicken' Salad

Try and eat an oyster mushroom whole, and they'll probably make you feel a bit sick, with their rich, earthy taste and spongy texture. But fine slice them and they miraculously turn into tender white meat, similar to chicken, very succulent and not at all overpowering.

- 15 g/½ oz arame, soaked 10 mins
- 60 g/2 oz dried tomatoes (p 167)
- 2 bunches watercress
- 6 lettuce leaves
- 200 g/7 oz oyster mushrooms
- 60 g/2 oz mixed beansprouts (p 42)
- 60 g/2 oz silverskin onions
- 2 cloves garlic, crushed
- 1 tbsp tahini
- 1 tbsp flax oil
- 1 tbsp apple cider vinegar
- 1 tsp white miso
- 1 tbsp Seagreens (p 48)
- 1 tbsp water

Soak the arame. If you are using shop-bought dried tomatoes, you can half the amount, and soak them in the same water. Using scissors snip the watercress into bite-sized pieces, straight into the salad bowl. Shred the lettuce leaves and add them in. Fine slice the oyster mushrooms in a food processor or salad slicer, and add them to the mix, along with the beansprouts and onions. In a small bowl, using a hand whisk, blend the remaining ingredients together to make a dressing. By now your arame should be ready – drain it and add it to the salad bowl with the tomatoes. Pour the dressing over the salad, toss, and serve immediately: watercress wilts quickly.

■ ■ ■ ■ This is quite a substantial salad and would be enough on its own. If you want to add anything, some cauliflower crackers (p 152) would complement it nicely.

- ■ 10 mins
- ■ Food processor, blender
- ■ **Serves four**

■ Cabbage Medley

Red cabbage contains more nutrients than white cabbage, for instance at least six times the vitamin C. Sauerkraut is also a great source of vitamin C, as well as containing friendly bacteria which are good for the digestion.

- ■ Avo pesto (see p 75) or Nikki's Dressing from *Eat Smart Eat Raw*
- ■ 250 g/8 oz sauerkraut
- ■ 400 g/14 oz red cabbage
- ■ 400 g/14 oz green cabbage
- ■ 60 g/2 oz olives
- ■ 60 g/2 oz mixed beansprouts (see p 42)

Prepare the avocado pesto. Slice the red and green cabbage using the fine slicing plate on your food processor. Transfer to a mixing bowl. Add the sauerkraut, separating the strands out with a fork. Add the olives and beansprouts. Using a fork or salad servers, toss the salad in the pesto, making sure all ingredients are evenly distributed.

■ ■ ■ ■ This is really good served with parsnip rice (p 97).

- 15 mins
- Serves four

Mediterranean Salad

This is a very simple salad to prepare, but if you get fresh, seasonal ingredients it's a real winner. If you're not strictly raw, baby new potatoes are a wonderful treat if you buy the first of the English season in June. Peas aren't raw either: unless you buy them in their pods and shell them yourself, they are most certainly blanched. We use jars of organic peas.

- 500 g/1 lb baby new potatoes (optional)
- 500 g/1 lb cherry tomatoes
- 1 cucumber
- 2 yellow peppers
- 12 leaves Romaine lettuce
- 200 g/7 oz olives
- 200 g/7 oz green peas
- 4 tbsp olive oil
- 2 tbsp balsamic vinegar
- 1 tbsp nori flakes
- Pinch sea salt
- Pinch black pepper

If you are using potatoes, clean them, half them, and put them in a pan covered in water. Bring them to the boil, and simmer for 10–15 mins. Meanwhile, half the tomatoes and pop in a large salad serving bowl. Finely dice the cucumber, add to the bowl. Fine slice the peppers, and lettuce, in a food processor if you have one. Add to the bowl, along with all the remaining ingredients, including your new potatoes. Give everything a good toss, so they are nicely covered in oil and vinegar. Serve immediately.

■ ■ ■ ■ Balsamic vinegar is not raw, but it has such a delicious flavour it is a very handy thing to keep in your cupboard for making a plate of vegetable more interesting. When Reuben was about five, one of his friends would come over to play frequently, and always demand 'lettuce and balsamic vinegar' for lunch!

- ■ 5 mins
- ■ Blender
- ■ **Serves two**

■ Curried Okra

Okra is one of those foods people either love or hate, I am definitely in the former camp. When you cut it and either cook it or blend it up, it releases a sticky, glutinous substance and thickens the dish it's in.

- ■ 6 tomatoes
- ■ 2 tbsp dried tomatoes
- ■ 2 tbsp olive oil
- ■ 2 tsp curry powder
- ■ 250 g/8 oz okra

Blend up everything but okra. Chop the okra finely and add it in. If you have a Vitamix, blend it in on a 3 setting. The okra and tomatoes will amalgamate to produce an authentic Indian dish.

■ ■ ■ ■ Okra, also known as lady's fingers, is not only used in Indian catering, but is popular in African and Middle Eastern cuisine.

- 15 mins, 10 mins presoaking
- Food processor
- **Serves two**

Fennel and Leek Salad

Leeks are a wonderful addition to a raw dish, surprisingly mild and pleasant. I love the way the stems separate out into rings. Smaller ones are better, as they are sweeter and more delicate. You can use just about any dressing on this simple salad; a creamy choice such as 'avo pesto' (p 75) works well. If you're in a hurry, just chuck on a splash of olive oil and a sprinkle of sea salt and ground pepper.

- 15 g/½ oz wakame, soaked 10 mins
- 1 bulb fennel
- 1 leek
- ½ cucumber
- 30 g/1 oz beansprouts (p 42)
- Any dressing (p 73-82)

Soak the wakame in advance. Using the fine slicing blade on your food processor, slice the fennel, leek and cucumber. Transfer to a mixing bowl. Add the beansprouts and drained wakame. Mix evenly. Pour in your dressing, and toss. Serve immediately.

■ ■ ■ ■ The best and most popular make of sea vegetables is Clearspring, and their's is the wakame we usually use. You can pick some up cheaper in Asian grocers, but the quality is nowhere near the same.

- 10 mins, 8-12 hrs soaking
- Food processor
- **Serves four**

◼ Parsnip Rice

It was years before I realised that you could eat parsnips raw. Go on, try one, and take a bite. They have a distinctive sweet taste, but a woody texture which makes them hard work to chew, and not the sort of thing you'd nibble on, like a carrot. But if you cut them into small enough bits, you can bypass this challenge and enjoy their unique flavour. Also, check out the parsnip soup recipe on p 90.

- 15 g/^{1}/$_2$ oz wakame
- 120 g/4 oz cashews, soaked 8-12 hrs
- 4 parsnips
- 2 tbsp sesame oil
- 1 tbsp rice vinegar
- 1 lemon, juiced
- 1 tbsp date syrup
- 1 tbsp tamari

Snip the wakame into tiny pieces with scissors. Soak in filtered water for 10 mins while you prepare the other ingredients. Top and tail the parsnips, and chop them into chunks. Pop them in the food processor with the cashews, and process until they're about the size of rice grains. Transfer to the mixing bowl, add the remaining ingredients along with the drained wakame. Give it all a good stir, and serve within 24 hrs. (Store in the fridge if you don't serve immediately.)

◼ ◼ ◼ ◼ If you've tried wakame and aren't a fan, you could substitute dulse or sea spaghetti in this recipe instead.

- 20 mins, 8-12 hrs soaking
- Food processor, blender
- **Serves four**

Sweet Potato Satay

Sweet potatoes are another of those vegetables that you wouldn't immediately think of eating raw. But they are surprisingly good, a bit like a cross between a carrot and an apple. You can peel them and cut them into sticks and serve them with a dip, or try them grated as in this recipe. This is the satay sauce from *Eat Smart Eat Raw*. The dates bring out the sweetness of the potatoes.

- 150 g/5 oz almonds, soaked 8-12 hrs
- 60 g/2 oz fresh dates, pitted
- Juice 1 lemon
- 1 red chilli, stem and seeds removed
- 4 tbsp water
- 1 tbsp tamari
- 2 sweet potatoes
- 60 g/2 oz fresh coconut pieces (see p 77)

To make the satay sauce, put the almonds, dates, lemon juice, chilli and water in the blender, and blend to a cream. Scrub the potatoes (you don't need to peel them) and grate them, using a fine grater. Put them in a mixing bowl. Grate the coconut pieces, and add them to the bowl. Pour the sauce over and mix thoroughly.

■ ■ ■ ■ If you can't get fresh coconut, desiccated, creamed or even butter will do just fine.

- 10 mins
- Food processor
- **Serves four**

Spicy Beetroot and Hemp Salad

Beetroot is more commonly eaten cooked in this country, but it is fantastic raw too, with a delicious sweetness which is complemented by the apple in this salad.

- 500 g/1 lb beetroot
- 2 apples
- 2 tbsp hemp seeds
- 2 tbsp hemp oil
- 1 tsp chilli sauce

Top, tail and peel the beetroot. Slice the apple into quarters and remove the core. Using a coarse grater, grate the beetroot and apple. Put them in a mixing bowl, with the remaining ingredients and toss.

■ ■ ■ ■ Children like the natural sweetness of this dish, and the beetroot is a great source of iron, while they're getting lots of essential fatty acids in the hemp. Just omit the chilli and add a dash of extra agave or raw honey.

- 5 mins, 70 mins soaking
- No equipment needed
- **Serves two**

Porcini Mushrooms and Pesto

Dried porcini mushrooms have a rich deep earthy flavour which, when added to a salad can transform it from a humble lunch into something fit for royalty.

- Pesto (see p 74)
- 45 g/1¹/₂ oz dried porcini mushrooms
- 1 tsp olive oil
- 1 tsp tamari
- 1 tsp nutritional yeast flakes
- 2 tbsp hijiki
- 4 leaves lettuce
- 90 g/3 oz lamb's lettuce (mâche)
- 12 olives

Soak the porcini mushrooms in filtered water for 10 mins. Drain, and marinade in olive oil, tamari, and nutritional yeast flakes for one hour. Soak the hijiki in filtered water for 30 mins. If you haven't done so already, this would be a good time to prepare the pesto (p 74). (Or you can cheat, and use shop-bought – Carley's do a great organic and vegan variety.)

Once your pesto is prepared, and everything is soaked and ready, tear the lettuce into fine strips, and put in a serving bowl with the lamb's lettuce, and olives. Add the drained hijiki, and the mushrooms, which will have absorbed all the marinade. Spoon on the pesto, give it a good toss with the salad servers, and serve immediately.

■ ■ ■ ■ Porcinis are one of the most highly prized mushrooms for their gourmet taste. They grow mainly in Europe, and are usually sold dried.

- 10 mins
- Food processor
- **Serves four**

Oriental Coleslaw

Like raw stir fry! A good tip if you're craving some hot food is to create a semi-raw stir-fry by cooking some sturdier veg, like onions and cabbage, and then throwing some in at the end raw, like finely sliced carrots and broccoli. This is a good way to trick your body into thinking it's enjoying cooked food but still getting lots of raw goodies in there.

- 2 tbsp arame
- 3 carrots
- 3 Jerusalem artichokes
- 1 small onion
- 120 g/4 oz chick pea sprouts (p 42)
- 1 cm/$\frac{1}{2}$ in ginger, minced
- 1 clove garlic, minced
- 2 tbsp sesame oil
- 1 tbsp date syrup
- 1 tbsp tamari
- 1 tbsp rice vinegar

Soak arame in filtered water for 10 mins while you're preparing the vegetables. Top and tail the carrots and artichokes. Top, tail and peel the onion. Put them all through a coarse grater. Transfer to a mixing bowl and spoon on the remaining ingredients. Drain the arame and add it in. Give it a good mix around, and serve within a few hours.

■ ■ ■ ■ I love Jerusalem artichokes, but they are often overlooked. Kind of like apple flavoured radishes, they are crisp and crunchy, cleansing and refreshing, and make a welcome change to carrots or cabbage in any sort of coleslaw dish.

- 5 mins
- No equipment needed
- **Serves one**

■ Simple Salad

This was a favourite family dinner for ages - simple but irresistible. Serve with a slice of Essene bread and tahini for the perfect quick but satisfying tea.

- 3 leaves Cos lettuce
- 60 g/2 oz lamb's lettuce
- 2 tbsp sauerkraut
- 30 g/1 oz alfalfa sprouts
- 1 tbsp olives
- 1 tbsp seeds or nuts - whatever you favour
- 1 tbsp flax oil
- 1 tsp apple cider vinegar
- 2 tbsp Atlantic sea salad
- 1 tbsp nutritional yeast flakes
- 1 tsp kelp powder
- 1 tsp lecithin granules

Wash the lettuces (we wash and dry them in a salad spinner) and shred very fine. Put in the salad bowl with everything else and give it a good mix round, so all the sea salad is evenly coating the lettuce. Serve immediately.

■ ■ ■ ■ Lamb's lettuce is the family's favourite salad green. It comes by many names - corn salad, lamb's leaf, or sometimes mâche. It is sweet, tender, and very easy to eat in huge quantities!

- 5 mins, 12 hrs marinading, 8 hrs dehydrating
- Dehydrator
- **Serves two**

Courgette Chips

Potatoes were the last cooked food I stopped enjoying. It was years, maybe even a decade, before I could go past a chip shop in winter without lusting after some chips. Amazingly, the cravings stopped eventually, and now if I met you in a chip shop I would not even be tempted to sneak one off your plate. These are reminiscent of chips – greasy, covered in salt and vinegar, and, if you eat them straight out of the dehydrator, even warm.

- 500 g/1 lb (approx 3) courgettes
- 1 tbsp Balsamic vinegar
- 2 tbsp olive oil
- 1 tbsp tamari
- 2 tbsp Atlantic sea salad

Slice your courgettes into fat chunky chips by topping and tailing, slicing them in half widthways, and then slicing each half lengthways into quarters. Put them in a shallow bowl or serving dish, pour over the vinegar, oil and tamari, and toss in the sea salad. Marinade for twelve hours, stirring at regular intervals to make sure the courgettes are evenly coated. They should absorb most of the liquid. At the end of twelve hours, lift your chips separately onto the drying trays of your dehydrator. Any leftover marinade can be used as a salad dressing. Dry the chips for 6-8 hours. Eat warm straight from the dehydrator – they're not half as convincing as chips when they're cold.

■ ■ ■ ■ You say zucchini...it can often be confusing reading US recipe books and websites, so here's a quick run down. Zucchini = courgettes, collard greens = spring greens, calabrese = broccoli, cilantro = coriander, eggplant = aubergine, and jicaima still evades me.

- 15 mins, soaking 1 hr
- No equipment needed
- **Serves two**

■ Saturday Salad

It used to be a Saturday tradition to sit together as a family and share a big meal. We used to call it 'Saturday Dinner Party'; most often we would have this salad with some dips and crisps. Then a few hours later, we would have a light tea, usually just pudding or cake. I love this salad, because you can really pig out on it, eat until you're full, and still feel wonderfully light and virtuous afterwards.

- 1 oak leaf lettuce
- 1 avocado
- 1 small head broccoli
- 4 gherkins
- 30 g/1 oz hijiki, soaked 1 hr
- 2 tbsp curry crunch (p 162)
- 30 g/1 oz alfalfa sprouts
- 2 tbsp flax oil
- 1 tbsp balsamic vinegar
- 1 tbsp Seagreens (p 48)
- 1 tbsp lecithin granules
- 2 tbsp nutritional yeast flakes

Rinse and tear the lettuce, and pop it in a salad bowl. We use a salad spinner for lettuce to get it nice and dry. Half the avocado, remove the pit, score the flesh into cubes, and scoop them out into the bowl. Chop the broccoli into small florets, put them in the bowl. Slice the gherkins thinly, and add them in with the hijiki, curry crunch, and alfalfa. Give it a good mix around, then add the remaining ingredients and toss. Serve immediately.

■ ■ ■ ■ Red oakleaf is my favourite lettuce, but you can substitute whichever appeals. I very rarely go for the commonly found Iceberg, baby gem, or round lettuces which more often than not seem a bit insipid. We like the more robust Lollo Rosso, Radicchio, Batavia, or good old Romaine.

■ 10 mins, marinating 8-12 hrs
■ Food processor, blender
■ **Serves four**

■ Curried Parsnips

Parsnips have a natural sweetness which lend themselves surprisingly well to salad. Eaten as they are, they are woody and hard work. But grate and marinade them, as in this recipe, and you will be won over.

■ 4 parsnips
■ 1 avocado
■ Juice 1 lemon
■ 2 tsp cumin powder
■ 1 tbsp garam masala
■ 1/2 red chilli pepper, seeds removed

Top and tail the parsnips. Grate them finely. Scoop the flesh out of the avocado. Put it in the blender along with the remaining ingredients, and blend to a purée, adding a little water if needs be. Transfer the parsnips and dressing to a serving bowl, and toss. You can serve this salad straightaway if you wish, but if you have time, leave it in the fridge for at least a few hours, preferably a day, to allow the parsnip to tenderise.

■ ■ ■ ■ Grated parsnips are also delicious marinated in avo pesto (p 75).

- 10 mins, soaking 10 mins
- Food processor
- **Serves two**

■ Eat More Greens

Eat Your Greens is one of my favourite recipes from *Eat Smart Eat Raw*. Here's a new twist on an old favourite, as they say.

- 500 g/1 lb greens, e.g. kale, cavalo nero, turnip greens, sprouting broccoli
- 15 g/½ oz wakame, soaked 10 mins
- 250 g/8 oz sauerkraut
- 1 large or 2 small avocado
- 1 tbsp Seagreens
- 2 tbsp nutritional yeast flakes

Chop the greens into manageable pieces and put them in the food processor. Blitz them until they're as chopped as they can be. Add in the drained wakame and sauerkraut and process again, briefly, so they're mixed in. Scoop the flesh out of the avocado and add that into the mix, along with the Seagreens and yeast flakes. Process for a few minutes until there are no lumps of avocado left. Serve immediately.

■ ■ ■ ■ We are so lucky in this country to get all the fantastic quality green vegetables that we have, there's no excuse for them not forming a central part of our diet. Although at first you might find them a bit chewy eaten raw, you can mash them up as in this recipe, make them softer by massaging olive oil into the leaves, or juice them if you have a good quality juicer.

- 30 mins, sprouting, soaking 4-8 hrs
- Blender, food processor
- **Serves four**

Dahl

Dahl is an Indian lentil soup, traditionally made with red split lentils.
Split lentils don't sprout, so we use brown, green, or Puy lentils.
They are all easy to sprout, and when mixed together look very pretty.

- 500 g/1 lb mixed lentil sprouts (p 42)
- 4 tbsp olive oil
- 1 tbsp tamari
- 1 tsp cumin
- 2 cloves garlic
- 90 g/3 oz sesame seeds, soaked 4-8 hrs
- 2 lemons, juiced
- 1 small bunch coriander
- 500 ml/16 fl oz water
- 1 red pepper
- 2 carrots
- 150 g/5 oz cauliflower
- 1 small head broccoli

In the blender, put the lentil sprouts, olive oil, tamari, cumin, garlic,
sesame seeds, lemon juice, coriander and water. Blend to a thick
cream. This is your dahl. (If you add less water, it makes a kind of lentil
hummus you can eat as a dip.) Next, assemble your vegetables and
chop them roughly into small pieces, about the size of cashew nuts.
You can do this by hand, using the S-blade on a food processor, or with
your Vitamix on a slow setting. Transfer the dahl and the vegetables to a
large bowl, and stir everything around with a spoon so the vegetables
are evenly mixed in. Divide between four bowls, and serve immediately.

■■■■ Sprouted lentils are an excellent source of raw protein,
so this dish is especially good for athletes, children,
and breastfeeding mums.

- 10 mins
- Blender
- Serves two

Fattoush

My version of the classic Lebanese salad. I love zaatar, it is worth tracking down from a speciality grocer if you can. It's an aromatic mix of thyme, sumac, and sesame seeds which the Lebanese believe gives strength and calms the mind.

- 2 bunches watercress
- Small bunch mint
- Small bunch parsley
- 2 lemons, juiced
- 4 tbsp olive oil
- 1 tbsp liquid aminos
- 4 tomatoes
- ½ cucumber
- 1 tbsp zaatar

Make a pesto (see p 74) with the mint, parsley, lemon juice, olive oil and liquid aminos. Quarter the tomatoes and cube the cucumber. Chop the watercress, mix all together with the zaatar.

Most of the watercress in the UK is farmed in Hampshire and Dorset. It is grown in shallow gravel beds and needs a constant supply of fresh spring water – a mature bed can consume as much as 5,000 gallons of water an hour! It takes one to three months to grow, depending on the time of year.

- 15 mins, 4-8 hrs soaking
- Food processor, blender
- **Serves four**

Fennel and Hijiki Salad in Pumpkin Seed Mayo

I adore this salad. Fennel is one of my favourite vegetables; with its distinctive flavour, refreshing crispness, and unusual shape, you could never accuse fennel of being boring. The pumpkin seed mayo makes a gorgeous creamy contrast, so this salad manages to combine a feeling of being virtuous and sinful at the same time.

- 400 g/14 oz white cabbage
- 1 bulb fennel
- 30 g/1 oz hijiki, soaked 1 hr
- 120 g/4 oz pumpkin seeds, soaked 4-8 hrs
- 1 tbsp hemp oil
- 1 lemon, juiced
- 1 clove garlic
- 125 ml/4 fl oz water
- Sea salt and black pepper to taste

Slice the cabbage and fennel using a fine slicer. Transfer to a mixing bowl with the drained hijiki. Put the pumpkin seeds, hemp oil, lemon juice, garlic and water in the blender and blend for a few minutes until you have a thick cream. Spoon it over the vegetables; you will only need about two-thirds of it, just enough to cover them, not drown them. Reserve the rest of the mayo for another use, or dehydrate it. Serve immediately.

■ ■ ■ ■ Pumpkin seeds are such a storehouse of nutrition, we try and eat them every day, either on their own as a snack, in nut butter, or blended into a dip or a sauce. As well as being one of the richest dietary sources of zinc, they are an exceptionally good source of the amino acid tryptophan, which raises serotonin levels in the brain.

- 10 mins
- Food processor, blender
- **Serves two**

■ Red Cabbage and Apple

This is based on a German dish, traditionally made by braising the red cabbage and apple, and popular at Christmas. But as you're hopefully realising by now, any recipe worth its sea salt works just as well raw as it does heated.

- 250 g/8 oz red cabbage
- 2 apples
- 1 tbsp vinegar
- 1 tbsp olive oil
- 1 tbsp raisins

Shred the red cabbage, and transfer to a mixing bowl. Blend the apples, vinegar and olive oil to a purée. Stir into the red cabbage with the raisins. This salad can be left for a few hours or up to a day and the cabbage will tenderise slightly in the apple.

■ ■ ■ ■ This is an unusual mix of flavours – bitter cabbage, sweet apples and sour vinegar – which combines to great effect. If you like goji berries, you could use them as a substitute for the raisins.

- 5 mins
- Blender
- **Serves two**

Mashed Parsnips

This is my favourite way of eating raw parsnips, creamy and comforting, and so warming; you'll forget they're not cooked! You can dehydrate any leftovers to make parsnip crisps.

- 500 g/1 lb parsnips
- 4 tbsp olive oil
- 125 ml/4 fl oz water
- Sprinkle of sea salt

Chop the parsnips finely, add everything to the blender, and purée to a cream. This works best with either a high speed blender or a hand blender. Serve immediately.

■ ■ ■ ■ This works equally as well with celeriac instead of parsnip, or try half carrot and half parsnip.

- 10 mins, presoaking 8 hrs
- Food processor, blender
- **Serves four**

■ Christmas Coleslaw

Is it possible to have Christmas dinner without Brussels sprouts? Only if you're a spoilsport. In all honesty, Brussels aren't great raw, a bit too crunchy and hard work for the jaws. But grated in this salad as a replacement for cabbage they make fantastic fresh and original coleslaw.

- 30 g/1 oz arame, soaked 10 mins
- 2 carrots
- 1 apple
- 1/2 onion
- 200 g/7 oz Brussels sprouts
- 60 g/2 oz chestnuts (precooked from a tin or jar)
- 60 g/2 oz peas
- 120 g/4 oz cashews, soaked 8-12 hrs
- 1 lemon, juiced
- 1 tsp white miso
- Water

Soak the arame. Top and tail the carrots. Quarter the apples and remove the core. Finely grate the carrots, apple, onion, and Brussels. Transfer to a mixing bowl with some good quality chestnuts, the peas, and arame. To make the mayonnaise, blend the cashews, lemon juice, miso and water. Toss the vegetables in the mayonnaise. This salad will keep for a day or two, and the vegetables will soften and the flavours improve.

■ ■ ■ ■ Brussels sprouts belong to the Brassica family of vegetables, like cauliflower, cabbage and broccoli, and contain high amounts of the phytonutrient sulphur.

- 15 mins
- Food processor, blender
- **Serves two**

Jane's Curry

This was sent to me by a friend of a friend. It's so easy to do, and really tasty.

- 2 avocados
- 2 lemons, juiced
- 2 tbsp sesame oil
- 1 tbsp curry powder
- 4 carrots
- 1 apple
- 90 g/3 oz fine green beans
- 1 red onion
- 2 stalks celery
- 1 red pepper
- 60 g/2 oz pine nuts
- 30 g/1 oz raisins

Start by making the curry sauce. Remove the flesh from the avocados and put it in the blender. Add the lemon juice, sesame oil, and curry powder and blend to a cream. If it won't turn over, add a little water to get it to a creamy consistency. Next prepare your vegetables. Grate the carrot and apple and transfer to a mixing bowl. Fine slice the green beans, onion, celery and red pepper, and add them to the bowl. Add the pine nuts, raisins, and avocado mixture and give it all a good stir. Serve immediately.

■ ■ ■ ■ In Ayurvedic medicine, they recommend you rinse your mouth with a tablespoon of raw sesame oil daily, to cleanse the whole body and expel toxins and pathogens. They say it helps to protect the body against colds and flus.

- 10 mins
- Food processor, blender
- **Serves four**

■ Creamy Cucumber and Apple

The freshness of the cucumber and mint in this salad contrasts exotically with the creamy sweet avocado dressing.

- 1 cucumber
- 1 apple
- 120 g/4 oz sweetcorn kernels
- 1 bunch mint
- 1 avocado
- 4 fresh dates, pitted
- 1 lemon, juiced
- 2 tsp white miso
- 4 tbsp water

Top and tail the cucumber, and grate it using a coarse grater. Core the apple and coarse grate that too. Put both in the mixing bowl, along with the corn kernels. Remove the mint leaves from the stems; discard the stems, put the leaves in the blender. Scoop the flesh out of the avocado, and put that in the blender too, with the dates, lemon juice, miso and water. Blend to a cream – add more water if you need to. Spoon the sauce over the cucumber mixture and give it a good stir. Serve immediately.

■ ■ ■ ■ Serving suggestion: serve with curried parsnips. This cooling cucumber and mint dish complements the heat of the curry.

- 10 mins, 1 hr soaking
- Food processor
- **Serves four**

Rocket and Hijiki

With green leaves more than anything else, it pays to get them fresh out of the ground. Salads that are sold bagged in supermarkets are likely to have been washed in chlorine and sprayed with chemicals to preserve them, even if they're certified organic (see the brilliant book *Not on the Label* by Felicity Lawrence). If you have the time and inclination, rocket is really easy to grow yourself.

- 30 g/1 oz hijiki, soaked 1 hr
- 200 g/7 oz rocket
- 60 g/2 oz dried tomatoes (p 167)
- 300 g/10 oz cauliflower pieces
- 120 g/4 oz silverskin onions
- 2 tbsp olive oil
- 1 tbsp balsamic vinegar
- 1 tsp tamari
- 1 tsp agave syrup

Wash the rocket, and using scissors, snip the leaves into bite-sized lengths and put them in the salad bowl. Add in your dried tomatoes. If you're using shop-bought ones, rather than home-made, soak them in water for 20-60 minutes first. Process the cauliflower in the food processor until it is in tiny granular pieces – I call this cauliflower snow, and often sneak it into salads so that the children won't notice they're eating cauliflower. Add it into the salad bowl, with the onions (any small pickled onion will do, but Biona are particularly good), the drained hijiki, and the dressing ingredients. Toss and serve immediately, before the rocket starts to wilt.

■ ■ ■ ■ Serving suggestion: served with red pepper ketchup and broccoli and cucumber crudités, this makes a substantial gourmet dinner in under half an hour.

- 10 mins
- Food processor
- **Serves four**

■ Broccoli Bliss

This has all my favourite things in.

- 60 g/2 oz broccoli bits (p 160)
- 4 small or 2 large broccoli heads
- 300 g/10 oz cauliflower
- 30 g/1 oz Atlantic sea salad
- 2 tbsp nutritional yeast flakes
- 1 tbsp Seagreens (p 48)
- 2 tbsp tahini
- 2 tbsp flax oil
- 1 lemon, juiced
- 1 tbsp apple cider vinegar

Prepare the broccoli and cauliflower by coarse chopping them, so they are in pieces about the same size as rice grains. Transfer to a serving bowl. Add in the broccoli bits, sea salad, nutritional yeast flakes and Seagreens. In a small bowl, whisk up the tahini, flax oil, lemon juice, and apple cider vinegar. When you have a nice creamy dressing, pour it over the salad and stir it in thoroughly. Serve within a couple of hours.

■ ■ ■ ■ Broccoli is such a staple in our house, we snack on it with dips, put it in our salads, make pâtés with it, stir it into soups, juice it, even coat it in raw chocolate and eat it - choccoli!

- 10 mins
- Blender
- **Serves two**

Egg Mayonnaise

When I was in junior school, one of my friends used to have egg mayonnaise sandwiches for lunch, and sometimes she would share them with me. And for some reason this dish reminds me of Katharine Vaziri's egg mayonnaise. You can spread it on Essene bread or crackers, but it's so good I eat it as it is.

- 300 g/10 oz cauliflower (about half a cauliflower)
- 1 large avocado
- 1 tbsp olive oil
- 1 clove garlic
- 2 tsp white miso
- 1 lemon, juiced

You want the cauliflower the size of rice grains; you can chop it up in the food processor, the Vitamix, or by hand. Transfer it to a mixing bowl. Remove the flesh from the avocado, and add it with all the remaining ingredients to the blender, to blend to a cream. Make sure there's no lumps of garlic in it; add water if you need to. Then transfer it to the bowl with the cauliflower and give it all a good stir together. Serve the same day.

■ ■ ■ ■ **Variation:** you can substitute some or all of the cauliflower for broccoli.

- 20 mins
- Spiral slicer
- **Serves four**

■ Noodles

These are amazingly authentic, like Chow Mein. They are also very satisfying, you don't need to eat too many. Why is it everyone knows you can eat raw carrots, but people don't think of eating the other root vegetables raw? Squash is a good British vegetable to add to your raw repertoire.

- 2 tbsp arame
- 1 medium-sized butternut squash
- 2 tbsp sesame seeds
- 2 tbsp poppy seeds
- 4 tbsp olive oil
- 1 tbsp tamari
- 120 g/4 oz sweetcorn kernels
- 16 cherry tomatoes, halved

Soak the arame in filtered water for 10–15 mins while you prepare the squash. Top and tail it, then slice it into half, the round bulbous end and the narrower neck. Slice the neck lengthways into quarters. Slice the round end in half and scoop out the seeds, then slice it in half again. You should now have eight pieces of squash. Using a spiral slicer on the noodle section, process each piece and transfer to a mixing bowl. Because of the unusual shape of the vegetable, you are likely to have odd ends leftover. Save these for another use: biscuits or soup. If you don't have a spiral slicer (or you are in a hurry) simply grate the squash. Add the remaining ingredients into the mixing bowl, along with the drained arame, and toss. You can serve as it is, or this also works well in pasta sauce (see p 142)

■ ■ ■ ■ Squash is a member of the cucurbit family, which includes cucumber, marrow, melon, pumpkin, gherkin, and loofah.

- 10 mins
- Food processor
- **Serves four**

■ Sweetheart Salad

Happiness in a salad! The bright colours and sweet flavours of this dish are guaranteed to put a smile in your belly, especially in autumn when the nights are starting to draw in and raw food is maybe seeming a little more challenging.

- 1 apple
- 1 beetroot
- 4 carrots
- ½ sweet potato
- 2 tbsp macadamia nuts
- 120 g/4 oz sweet corn kernels
- 4 tbsp mirin
- 2 tbsp sesame oil
- 1 tbsp Chinese 5 spice

Prepare your vegetables: remove the core of the apple, peel the beetroot, and top and tail the carrots. Along with the sweet potato, cut into chunks ready for use, and chop the size of rice granules. You can do this in a food processor with the S-blade, in a Vitamix, or by hand. Stir in the remaining ingredients. Eat straight away, or marinade for a few hours first.

■ ■ ■ ■ Macadamias are native to Australia, and are hard to find in the UK and generally pricey. But they are one of the tastiest, creamiest nuts around, with an unusual flavour and satisfying crunch.

- 20 mins
- Blender, food processor
- **Serves two**

Thai Red Curry

Fresh coconut makes this rich and creamy and very warming with all those spices. Thai spices are easier to find now, supermarkets often stock a selection. If you can't get fresh coconut, you can substitute creamed coconut or coconut milk, but neither of these is raw.

- 2 tbsp arame
- 4 red peppers
- 2 tomatoes
- 1 stick celery
- 1 stick lemongrass
- Small bunch coriander
- 1 lime
- 120 g/4 oz fresh coconut pieces
- 4 fresh dates, pitted
- 2 cloves garlic
- 2 cm/1 in galangal
- 8 cup mushrooms
- 8 baby corn
- 45 g/1$\frac{1}{2}$ oz mung bean or lentil sprouts

Prepare the arame by soaking it for 10-15 mins. Remove the stem and seeds from the red pepper – chop into eighths. Top and tail the carrots, and chop into chunks. Quarter the tomatoes. Chop the celery into chunks. Chop the lemongrass and coriander, juice the lime. Put the peppers, carrots, tomatoes, celery, lemongrass, coriander, lime juice, coconut, dates, garlic and galangal in the blender. The liquid from the vegetables should be plenty to make a thick sauce. Fine slice the mushrooms and baby corn, and transfer them to a mixing bowl with the beansprouts, and the drained arame. Pour the red sauce over, and give it a good mix, making sure it's evenly stirred. Serve garnished with a sprig of fresh coriander for a meal fit for the King of Thailand himself.

■ ■ ■ ■ Baby corn is mainly grown in Thailand, and is cultivated by harvesting standard corn plants early, before they are mature.

- ■ 5 mins
- ■ No equipment
- ■ **Serves one**

■ My Favourite Things

Just a few of...**Perfect light lunch for the woman on the run.**

- ■ 30 g/1 oz dulse
- ■ 30 g/1 oz alfalfa
- ■ 10 pitted olives
- ■ 60 g/2 oz rocket
- ■ 1 tbsp hemp oil
- ■ 1 tsp liquid aminos
- ■ 1 tsp agave
- ■ 1 tsp lemon juice

Rinse the dulse. Toss everything together in a bowl. Delicious served with rye bread (p 151) spread with pumpkin seed butter.

■ ■ ■ ■ Alfalfa when fully grown is similar to hay, and is the third most widely grown crop in the US. Its primary use is as animal feed for cattle, sheep and horses.

- 15 mins
- Food processor
- **Serves four**

■ Kohl Rabi Coleslaw

Also known as turnip cabbage, this white bulbous root vegetable has a sweet crunch that makes it a great candidate for coleslaw. Usually white, you can also sometimes find pretty purple ones too.

- 60 g/2 oz sea spaghetti
- 2 kohl rabi, grated
- 2 large carrots
- 1 onion
- 1 small cauliflower
- 1 avocado
- 1 tbsp Seagreens (p 48)
- 2 tbsp nutritional yeast flakes
- 1 tbsp apple cider vinegar
- 2 tbsp hemp oil

Rinse the sea spaghetti, and soak in water for a few minutes to remove any excess salt. Top and tail the kohl rabi and carrots. Peel and quarter the onion. Grate the kohl rabi, carrots, onion and transfer to a mixing bowl. To prepare the cauliflower, take the heads and process them in a food processor with the S-blade until it's ground up into tiny pieces like snowflakes - we call this 'cauliflower snow', it's a great addition to any salad and a good way to include cauliflower in your food if you're not keen on eating it in big chunks. Add the cauliflower to the mixing bowl. Cube the avocado flesh, and add that to the bowl. Sprinkle on your Seagreens, yeast flakes, vinegar and hemp oil and give it all a good mix up. Can be eaten straight away or left to marinade for a few hours.

■■■■ Michigan in the USA claims to be the kohl rabi capital of the world, and even holds kohl rabi festivals!

■ Savouries

Most of these recipes call for a dehydrator. If you feel sure you're going to be experimenting with raw foods for more than a few months, it's worth getting one of these 'raw ovens', you'll have loads of fun making biscuits and burgers for you and your family. If you haven't got a dehydrator there are a few options available to you.

You can lightly fry burgers in coconut oil (the only cold-pressed oil which is heat stable and so most suitable for frying). Just a few minutes on each side will warm them up and help them stick together without cooking them.

You can place them under a low grill for a few minutes on each side. Again, make sure they're lightly toasted on both sides without being cooked through.

You can put them in an airing cupboard or on top of a hot radiator for a day. This will dry them out a little.

If it's hot, you can try sun-drying. Leave them out in the sun for a day, but make sure the flies don't get on them, and bring them in if it starts to rain.

Rawfooders often advise using the oven on the lowest heat with the door open. Just be careful not to leave it unattended, and make sure the oven doesn't get too hot.

However you choose to prepare them, the dishes in this section make a substantial addition to any meal and a welcome alternative to simple salads.

- 20 mins, soaking 8-12 hrs, drying 12 hrs
- Blender, dehydrator
- **Makes 12 burgers**

Spicy Almond Burgers

Flax seeds are probably the best way of binding foods together in raw food cuisine. A tablespoon or two of ground seeds is the surest way to help your mixture stick together when you're making burgers, loaves, pastries, biscuits, anything that needs a bit of firming up.

- 2 tbsp flax seeds, ground
- 2 carrots
- 3 tomatoes
- 2 sticks celery
- 1 onion
- 2 red chillies
- 1 tbsp tamari
- 250 g/8 oz almonds, soaked 8–12 hrs

Grind the flax seeds in a coffee grinder or high power blender. Roughly chop the carrots, tomatoes, celery, and onion so they fit in your blender. Remove the seeds and stem from the chilli, and add that to the blender too, as well as the almonds and tamari. Turn the blender on and purée until you have no odd lumps of vegetable or nut left. Then add the flax seeds and blend again. Shape into patties with your hands, not more than about 2 cm/1 in thick and about 10 cm/4 in in diameter. It should make about twelve burgers. Put them on the drying trays, and dry for 12 hrs, until crunchy on both sides, but tender in the middle.

■ ■ ■ ■ Flax seeds are also the easiest way to make raw crackers. Simply soak your seeds in water, and when they've absorbed as much as they are able (usually about three times as much, weight for weight), then add your favourite flavourings, sweet or savoury, spread thinly onto dehydrator sheets, and dry until crispy.

- 20 mins, soaking 8-12 hrs, dehydrating 6 hrs
- Blender, dehydrator
- **Serves four (makes about 16)**

Beetroot Burgers

Even people who don't like beetroot love these. The dehydrating process brings out the natural sweetness of this wondrous vegetable.

- 2 tbsp flax seeds, ground
- 4 beetroot
- 1 large carrot
- 1 tomato
- 1 red chilli
- 1/2 onion
- 4 fresh dates, pitted
- 150 g/5 oz almonds, soaked 8-12 hrs
- 1 tbsp tamari
- 125 ml/4 fl oz water

Grind the flax seeds in a coffee grinder or high power blender. Top, tail and peel the beetroot, top and tail the carrot, and chop them into bite-sized chunks. Cut the tomato into quarters. Remove stem and seeds from the chilli. A high powered blender will work best, otherwise use a food processor. Put in all the ingredients apart from the flax seeds. You won't get a purée, more of a mush. When you're confident there's no lumps of vegetable left in (you may get the odd stubborn bit of carrot or beetroot, just remove it), add the flax seeds, these will bind the mixture. Shape into patties about 2 cm/1 in high and 10 cm/4 in wide. They should fill two drying trays. Dry for 4 hrs, flip over, and dry for a further 2 hrs. Eat within 24 hrs. These are lovely burgers, moist and substantial. Serve with ketchup or mayonnaise and a side salad.

■ ■ ■ ■ Flax seed tea is beneficial for the colon, strengthening and cleansing. Soak 1 tbsp of seeds in 600 ml of water, simmer for 10 minutes, strain and drink. Add lemon juice and raw honey if you want to improve the taste.

- 15 mins, soaking 4-8 hrs, drying 12 hrs
- Blender, dehydrator
- **Makes 18 burgers**

Sunny Burgers

From the beautiful sunflower plant, sunflower seeds are probably the most popular seed to snack on. They're a great source of vitamin E, essential fatty acids, magnesium and selenium.

- 250 g/8 oz sunflower seeds, soaked 4-8 hrs
- 2 tbsp flax seeds, ground
- 2 sticks celery
- 1 onion
- 3 tomatoes
- 1 red chilli
- 3 carrots, chopped
- 1 tbsp tamari

Soak sunflower seeds in advance. Grind flax in a coffee grinder or high power blender. Chop the celery, onion, and tomatoes. Remove the stem and seeds from the chilli pepper. Put everything bar the flax seeds in the blender. Blend to a thick purée, and then add the flax seeds in to stiffen the mixture. Using a tablespoon, spoon dollops of the mixture on to the dehydrator tray, and flatten down to about 2-3 cm/1-1$^1/_2$ in fat and 10 cm/4 in in diameter. Arrange on a drying tray and dry for 8 hrs. Flip and dry for a further 4 hrs.

■ ■ ■ ■ I am often asked if flax seeds on their own are sufficient to fulfil your EFA requirements. Two tablespoons of flax contain well over the RDA, but unless we have an extremely efficient digestive system, the body finds it hard to extract the necessary substances from the seeds, so I always advise supplementing with oils.

- 15 mins, 8–12 hrs soaking, 12 hrs dehydrating
- Blender, dehydrator
- **Makes 12**

Love Burgers

These are beautifully sweet and creamy, and a wonderful romantic pink. Serve them on Valentine's Day, or for a special lover's meal.

- 250 g/8 oz cashews, soaked 8-12 hrs
- 2 red peppers
- 1 small cauliflower
- 1/2 onion
- 2 tsp white miso

Soak the cashews in advance. Prepare the peppers: remove stem and seeds and chop into large chunks. Remove leaves from the cauliflower and chop the florets into chunks. Put everything in the blender and blend to a thick cream. You shouldn't need water, as the peppers will turn to liquid. Take heaped tablespoons of the mixture and, using your hands, mould them into love heart shapes on the drying tray – about 2 cm/1 in high and 10 cm/4 in in diameter. Place on a drying tray and dehydrate for 12 hrs, turning about two-thirds of the way through. Serve with red pepper ketchup drizzled around the plate to complete the effect.

■ ■ ■ ■ We prefer white miso, or shiro miso, because it is less salty and has a gentler flavour. But experiment with the other types of miso, like mugi and hatcho. Natto miso is a chutney which makes a delicious accompaniment to salads or can be used in dressings.

- 15 mins, soaking 4-8 hrs, drying 18 hrs
- Blender, dehydrator
- **Makes 12**

Hemp Burgers

Hemp seeds lend a distinctive depth to any dish. They are one of the best sources of the essential fats Omega 3 and Omega 6, as well as the hard to find gamma-linoleic acid.

- 120 g/4 oz sunflower seeds, sprouted (see p 42)
- 120 g/4 oz hemp seeds, soaked 4-8 hrs
- 4 tomatoes
- 1 red pepper
- Small bunch parsley
- 1 onion
- 1 tbsp garam masala

Sprout your sunflower seeds a day or two in advance. Pre-soak your hemp seeds. Prepare your vegetables for the blender: remove any unwanted stems, stalks and seeds, and chop into large chunks. Put all the ingredients in and blend to a thick pink cream. Spoon it out onto drying trays, making patties, about 3 cm/1¹/₂ in fat and 10 cm/4 in wide. Dry for 12 hrs, then flip them over and dry for another 6 hrs.

■ ■ ■ ■ Hemp is not only a fantastic food, it's brilliant to put
on the skin too, healing, strengthening and rejuvenating.
Our favourite bodycare brand is the Yaoh range, all vegan,
all natural, and all hemp based.

- 15 mins, 4-8 hrs soaking, 12 hrs drying
- Blender, dehydrator
- **Makes 12**

Lentil Burgers

Sprouted lentils are a great source of protein, and help to stabilise blood sugar levels. They are rich in B vitamins and hard to find trace minerals like molybdenum and manganese. We usually use green lentils, but you can use the small black Puy lentils too. Red lentils will not sprout as they have been cracked.

- 200 g/7 oz lentils, sprouted (see p 42)
- 120 g/4 oz sunflower seeds, soaked 4-8 hrs
- 60 g/2 oz flax seeds, ground
- 1 onion
- Small bunch parsley
- Small bunch basil
- 4 tbsp olive oil
- 1 tbsp miso
- 4 tbsp water

Sprout your lentils two or three days in advance. Pre-soak your sunflower seeds. Grind your flax seeds in a coffee grinder or high power blender. Prepare the onion, parsley and basil by chopping them loosely and put them in the blender. Put everything else in apart from the flax seeds and process to thick batter. You may need to add a little more water. Add the flax seeds in and blend again until the mixture has thickened. Shape into patties with your hands. With a spoon, shape into burgers about 3 cm/1½ in high and 10 cm/4 in wide on your drying trays. Dry for 12 hrs.

■ ■ ■ ■ Onions and garlic are avoided by many yogis and Buddhists because they are said to be over-stimulating, or 'rajasic' in the Ayurvedic system, and not conducive to meditation.

- 30 mins, soaking 4-8 hrs, dehydrating 12 hrs
- Blender, dehydrator
- **Serves four**

■ Tempura

I used to adore tempura; it was one of my favourite treats. An Asian dish, it is made by coating fresh vegetables in batter and deep-frying them. One time we visited a Thai restaurant with the family, and I was determined to recreate some raw tempura at home. After a bit of trial and error, this is what I came up with. Serve warm, straight from the dehydrator, with some dipping sauce (p 57).

- 60 g/2 oz sunflower seeds, soaked 4-8 hrs
- 60 g/2 oz pumpkin seeds, soaked 4-8 hrs
- 4 red peppers
- 4 Portobello mushrooms
- 60 g/2 oz flax seeds
- 1 red chilli, stem and seeds removed
- 2 cloves garlic
- 2 fresh dates, pitted
- 1 tbsp tamari
- 500 ml/16 fl oz water

You can pre-soak your sunflower and pumpkin seeds in the same bowl together. Remove the stem and seeds from the pepper. Slice lengthways into strips about 1 cm/1/2 in wide. Slice the mushrooms into similar size pieces. To make the batter, put all the ingredients bar the peppers and mushrooms in the blender and process for a few minutes, until the mixture starts to thicken. It should be kind of elastic. Transfer the batter and the mushrooms and peppers to a mixing bowl, and mix thoroughly so they are completely coated. Spread the mix over three or four drying trays, making sure it is thinly and evenly distributed. Dry for 12 hrs.

■ ■ ■ Tempura was originally introduced to Japan by the Portuguese in the 15th century, and the name is said to derive from the Portuguese word temporo which means seasoning.

- 5 mins, 4-8 hrs soaking, 18 hrs drying
- Blender, dehydrator
- **Makes 18**

Spinach Cakes

Spinach is an amazing source of nutrients, full of cancer-beating flavonoids and carotenoids, and vitamins and minerals. One cup of spinach contains 200 % of the RDA of vitamin K, which is important to help maintain bone health. If you can track down loose spinach rather than the cut and bagged leaves, it is much tastier and more nutritious.

- 90 g/3 oz sesame seeds, soaked 4-8 hrs
- 250 g/8 oz spinach
- 1 tsp tamari
- 1 tsp kelp
- 1/2 onion
- 125 ml/4 fl oz water

This is one of those easy peasy recipes. Pre-soak your sesame seeds. Then just chuck everything in the blender, and whiz for a couple of minutes, until all the seeds are ground in. Then spoon dollops of the mixture onto drying trays, and dry for 12 hrs. Turn and dry on the other side for a further six hours.

■ ■ ■ ■ These little patties are particularly good served with Lemon Pickle (p 63) or Date Chutney (p 62).

- 5 mins, 4-8 hrs soaking, 12 hrs drying
- Blender, dehydrator
- **Makes four**

■ Coriander Wraps

These are one of those simple things you can make which transforms a humble salad into something spectacular. Even if you've only got a few lettuce leaves in the fridge and a jar of tahini in the cupboard, wrap them in one of these and you'll have a feast.

- 150 g/5 oz flax seeds, soaked in 500 ml (16 fl oz) water for 4-8 hrs
- 1/2 onion
- Small bunch coriander
- 1 tbsp cumin powder
- 1 tbsp garam masala

Soak the flax seeds in the water; they will absorb it all and become gelatinous. If you haven't got 4 hrs, even 20 mins will do – you'll still need to add the full 500 ml (16 fl oz) of water to your mixture. Once they're ready pop them in the blender with all the other ingredients. Blend to a purée, until there are no seeds discernable in the mix. Take a quarter of the mixture, and spread it in a round onto a drying tray. Your round will nearly fill the tray – about 30 cm/12 in diameter. Make three more rounds, and dry for 8 hrs. Flip over, and dry for another 4 hrs. Don't let them go crispy – you want them to be nice and pliable, so you can fold them over. If you notice them start to go crispy round the edge, take them out straight away. Slide each round onto a plate. Spread with a dip, pâté, or some nut butter. Heap your favourite salad on top in a semi-circle, so only one side is covered. Then fold the wrap in half across the middle, and eat like pita bread. Very satisfying. These will keep for a couple of days if needs be.

■ ■ ■ ■ You can just cram your wrap with lettuce, olives and alfalfa, or try Rocket and Hijiki (p 115) or Broccoli Bliss (p 116).

- 10 mins, 4-8 hrs soaking, 18 hrs dehydrating
- Blender, dehydrator
- **Makes 24**

■ Bean Cakes

These go great with one of the chutneys on p 61-63. You can use a mix of lentils, aduki, mung beans, sunflower seeds or chick peas in this recipe. If you haven't been organised enough to sprout your own, one of the ready-made bags of mixed sprouts available in wholefood stores is perfect.

- 250 g/8 oz mixed beansprouts (p 42)
- 90 g/3 oz sesame seeds, soaked 4-8 hrs
- Small bunch coriander
- 1 onion
- 2 tbsp olive oil
- 1 tbsp cumin powder
- 1 tbsp garam masala
- 1 tbsp tamari

Sprout your beans in advance. Pre-soak your sesame seeds. Prepare the coriander and onion for the blender. Put all the ingredients in and blend to a thick purée. Add a little water if it won't blend, but keep it as thick as possible. Spoon dollops of the mixture onto a drying tray – about a tablespoon at a time. Ideally, they want to be 1-2 cm/½-1 in high – any fatter and they won't dry out. Dry for 12 hrs, turn and dry for 6 hrs more. Will keep stored in an airtight container in the fridge for up to one week.

■ ■ ■ ■ Coriander is the only plant to be classified as a herb and a spice. The leaves are referred to as a herb, while the seeds are used as a spice.

- 10 mins, 18 hrs drying
- Blender, dehydrator
- **Makes 12 sausages**

■ Lentil and Sage Sausages

Very traditional! Great for lunches and picnics.

- 90 g/3 oz lentils, sprouted (see p 42)
- 1 onion
- Small bunch sage
- 4 tbsp olive oil
- 60 g/2 oz sesame seeds, soaked 4-8 hrs
- 30 g/1 oz dried tomatoes
- 1 tbsp miso

Sprout your lentils two or three days in advance. Peel, top and tail the onion and quarter it ready for the blender. Chop the sage loosely, and put everything in the blender. When you have a thick purée, take out about one tablespoon at a time and form into fat sausages on the trays, about 2cm/1 in in diameter and 10 cm/4 in long. Place on drying trays and dry for 12 hrs. Turn and dry for a further 6 hrs. Serve with tomato ketchup (*Eat Smart Eat Raw*) or red pepper ketchup (p 55).

■ ■ ■ ■ The Latin name for sage is *salvia officinalis*, which is derived from *salvere*, the Latin for 'to be saved', because of its reputation as a medicinal plant.

- 10 mins, 4-8 hrs soaking, 12 hrs drying
- Blender, dehydrator
- **Serves four**

■ Chick Pea Loaf

Sprouted chick peas are a very calming, soothing and reassuring food when blended into loaves, hummus or soups. Just be careful when sprouting to keep the tails small: you want to have the bean bigger than the tail or you'll get a not so pleasant, woody flavour to your recipe. Keep a little tail and you'll barely be able to tell the difference between a raw hummus and a cooked one.

- 150 g/5 oz chick peas, sprouted (see p 42)
- 90 g/3 oz sesame seeds, soaked 4-8 hrs
- 2 carrots
- 1 onion
- 4 tbsp olive oil
- 1 small bunch parsley, finely chopped
- 2 tsp miso
- 8 tbsp water
- Pasta sauce (p 140) (optional)

Sprout your chick peas two or three days in advance. Pre-soak your sesame seeds. Top and tail the carrots and onion, and prepare them for the blender. Put all the ingredients in and blend to a thick purée. Spoon out onto a drying tray, and shape into a loaf about 3 cm/1¹/₂ in high, 15 cm/6 in wide, and 20 cm/8 in long. If you have the time and the inclination, make a serving of pasta sauce and spread it over the top. Dehydrate for 12 hrs. Otherwise, you can make the sauce when you are ready to serve it, and spoon it over like gravy. Or serve with red pepper ketchup (p 55).

■ ■ ■ ■ Chick peas are one of the top sources of dietary fibre, this dish contains virtually 100 % of the daily requirement.

- 15 mins
- Food processor
- **Serves four**

■ Mediterranean Stuffed Tomatoes

These are fun and easy to make, and are a great centrepiece for a summer lunch. It's the fresh herbs that add an extra dimension and make it a meal to savour. Goes well with Sweetheart Salad (p 119)

- 120 g/4 oz sunflower seeds, sprouted (p 42)
- 4 large beefsteak tomatoes
- 1 carrot
- 1 stick celery
- 1 bunch basil
- 1 bunch oregano
- 2 cloves garlic
- 1 tsp miso
- 1 lemon, juiced
- 2 tbsp olive oil
- 2 tbsp alfalfa sprouts (p 42)

Sprout your sunflower seeds for two or three days. Slice the tops off the tomatoes and set aside (you don't need the lids). Using a paring knife carefully cut out the centres of the tomatoes, leaving a 1 cm/¹/₂ in rim of flesh round the edge. Scoop out all the soft seedy innards with a spoon. You only need half of this pulp for the recipe; the rest you can save for a soup or sauce. Prepare the carrot, celery, basil and oregano by chopping them into chunks to fit into your food processor.
Pop them in, along with the sunflower sprouts, pulp of two tomatoes, garlic, miso, lemon juice and olive oil. Process them so they still have a granular texture, and the ingredients are not completely blended up. Spoon this mixture into the four tomatoes. Garnish with alfalfa and serve immediately.

■ ■ ■ ■ If you can't get fresh herbs, a dried blend of oregano, basil, rosemary and thyme is delicious in a different way.

- 15 mins, 8-12 hrs soaking, 8-10 hrs dehydrating
- Blender, dehydrator
- **Makes eight pancakes**

Cashew Pancakes

This is based on a recipe shared by a raw mum from England called Karen Rodgers. They're amazingly authentic – spread with agave syrup and white almond butter for a Shrove Tuesday treat. The temptation is to eat heaps of them, but it's probably wise to stick to two per person as they're very rich.

- 250 g/8 oz cashews, soaked 8-12 hrs
- 500 ml/16 fl oz water
- 2 tsp vanilla extract
- 1 tsp tamari
- 4 fresh dates, pitted
- 1 tbsp psyllium powder

Pre-soak your cashews. Put everything bar the psyllium in the blender and blend to a runny cream. Keep your blender on for a few minutes to ensure the mix is really smooth, not bitty. When it's ready, add the psyllium and blend again briefly. Spoon out on to drying trays immediately, before the psyllium starts to set. You can fit two pancakes to a tray, about 15 cm/6 in in diameter. Spread it fairly thin, and it should make eight pancakes. Dry for 6 hrs, then flip over and dry for another 2-4 hrs on the other side. Serve warm, straight out of the dehydrator. Leftovers (ha!) will keep for a day or two in the fridge.

■ ■ ■ ■ The cashew is the seed of the cashew apple fruit. Not commonly eaten in Europe or the US, the fruit is very popular in Brazil and the Caribbean.

- 40 mins, 8-12 hrs soaking, 2 hrs setting
- Food processor, blender
- **Serves eight**

■ Spinach and Mushroom Quiche

Raw pies and quiches are so much easier to make than cooked ones. I often demonstrate them at workshops and people are amazed at how quickly you can throw together such a tasty and impressive dish. No rolling out pastry, no pre-baking, no boiling sauces, no worrying about lumps or burnt crusts. Phew!

- 250 g/8 oz almonds
- 250 g/8 oz rolled oats
- 1 tbsp tahini
- 1 tbsp miso
- 1 tsp chilli powder
- 1 tsp cumin powder
- 1 tbsp water
- 8 mushrooms (120 g/4 oz)

- 250 g/8 oz spinach
- 1 carrot
- ½ onion
- ½ avocado
- 1 tsp tamari
- 2 tbsp olive oil
- 125 ml/4 fl oz water
- 1 tbsp psyllium

First, make the crust. Put the almonds and oats in a food processor and process as fully as possible. Add the tahini, miso, chilli, cumin and process again. If the mixture isn't sticking together, add a little water; a tablespoon should be sufficient. When it's formed sticky dough, press it into a large flan tin, lining the sides and base. Next, finely slice the mushrooms and arrange them evenly in the pastry case. To make the spinach cream, prepare the spinach, carrot, onion and avocado, and put them in the blender. Add the tamari, olive oil, and water and blend. Once you have a thick cream, add the psyllium and blend again.
 The mixture will start to thicken. Pour it over the mushrooms, filling the almond pastry case. Pop it in the fridge for a couple of hours to allow the psyllium to set. Serve with a green salad like Rocket and Hijiki (p 115).

■ ■ ■ ■ Cumin seeds are quite different from the powder. The seeds taste similar to fennel and dill, and are a super addition to salads and soups. The powder on the other hand is one of the predominant notes in curry powder and has a warming, uplifting aroma and taste.

- 30 mins
- Food processor, blender
- **Serves eight**

Tomato Quiche

- 300 g/10 oz almonds
- 150 g/5 oz rolled oats
- 1 tbsp tahini
- 1 tbsp miso
- 2-4 tbsp water
- 8 mushrooms (250 g/8 oz)
- 90 g/3 oz olives
- 1 corn cob
- 5 tomatoes
- 1 carrot
- 1 stick celery
- 2 tbsp dried toms (p 167)
- 2 dates
- 1/4 onion
- 1 tsp tamari
- 1 tbsp olive oil
- 1 tbsp apple cider vinegar
- 1 bunch basil
- 1 tbsp psyllium

Grind the almonds and oats in a high power blender or coffee grinder. Transfer to a mixing bowl and add tahini, miso and water. Knead with your hands until you have firm dough. Press this into a large flan tin, lining the base and sides with a crust about 1 cm/1/2 in thick. Next prepare your filling. Slice the mushrooms into pieces about 1/2 cm/1/4 in thick. Arrange the pieces over your flan base. Sprinkle over the olives. Strip the corn kernels off the cob with a knife, and sprinkle those over the mushrooms and olives. The final step is to make the tomato sauce. Prepare your tomatoes, carrots and celery for the blender, and blend up with the dried tomatoes, dates, onions, tamari, olive oil, vinegar and basil. Blend to a smooth purée. Add the psyllium and blend again. The psyllium will start to set pretty quickly, so pour it over the flan base immediately. Leave for an hour or two in the fridge to set and serve with a green salad like Simple Salad (p 102). Will keep for three or four days in the fridge.

■ ■ ■ ■ The French name for tomato is *pomme d'amour*, or apple of love, because they attribute aphrodisiacal qualities to the fruit.

■ Pasta sauce

My all-time favourite recipe is pasta sauce. Every raw chef has their own pasta sauce recipe, and you may think there can't be much to it, just chuck some tomatoes and basil in the blender, and there you have it. But believe me, there is something about this recipe that is unbeatable. No matter how many times I make it, I always end up scraping the bowl and licking the jug to get every last precious drop out. It was also one of the first recipes I ever developed. My three-year-old son was a very picky raw eater (note to other mums with the same problem: it was a phase, it passes, just stick with it). So I had to invent ways of hiding raw foods in his dinner that he would find palatable. One of his favourite dinners was wheat-free pasta drowned in this sauce.

Obviously, the main ingredients are tomatoes – some fresh and some dried. You can either buy sun-dried in packets, or dry them yourself in the dehydrator; I prefer to dry them myself because a) then I know they're really raw, and relatively fresh, and b) it's cheaper. Dried tomatoes add a real richness and depth of flavour to any sauce. Then I add carrot and celery, as a way of adding body to the sauce, and sneaking some extra veg into my children's bodies. They would refuse to eat celery in its natural state, but they get plenty this way, hidden in sauces and the like. I also put in a handful of dulse, and a little kelp. We eat tons of sea veg, it's so important as a source of minerals, and is a wonderfully satisfying addition to savoury dishes. Did you know dulse has fifteen times more calcium than cow's milk, weight for weight? Next in the blender are dates and onion. For some reason, this unlikely pair of ingredients really work together; creating a mouth-watering blend of sweet and spice. Finally, you want a little apple cider vinegar, a dash of tamari, and a drizzle of olive oil, to ensure a vibrant, tangy sauce.

We have it every week, because the variations are endless. If I'm serving it for the children, I would just leave it like that, and pour it over the pasta. Or sometimes they have 'baked beans': sprouted chick peas, which have been cooked in water for half an hour to soften them. But for my husband and I, I tweaked it a little, and transformed it into a whole new dish. For a basic pasta, I add a bunch of basil, half a red chilli, and a clove of garlic per person. Pour it over chopped veg, and serve with a sprinkling of your favourite raw cheese substitute, or a handful of pine nuts. Try courgetti (courgettes done in the spiral slicer like spaghetti), or carrotelli (carrots done in the spiral slicer like tagliatelli). Butternut squash also makes great noodles, when done in the spiral slicer. Another obvious one is to use it as a sauce on a pizza base. There are plenty of raw pizza base recipes around; you could try simply whizzing up tomatoes and flax seeds, then shape the mix into thin rounds, and dehydrate. If you haven't got time to make bases, mix the usual pizza toppings into the sauce – sweetcorn, mushrooms, and olives, say, and use to stuff peppers – pizza peppers! For a raw chilli, add one whole red chilli per person, and mix some finely grated beetroot and carrot into your sauce, along with a big handful of beansprouts. Fancy a curry? Add one clove of garlic, an equal-sized piece of ginger, one red chilli, and a teaspoon of curry powder. Mix in some veg – mushrooms, cauliflower, broccoli and red pepper is a good combination. And finally, my favourite variation is Thai red curry: add in traditional Thai seasonings, such as galangal, lime, lemongrass, coriander, and coconut (for the full list, see my book *Eat Smart Eat Raw*).

By my count, that makes eleven different ways to use this sauce, and there are bound to be others you can think of.

- 10 mins
- Blender
- **Serves one**

■ Basic Recipe for Pasta Sauce

- 3 tomatoes
- 1 carrot
- 1 stick celery
- 1 tbsp dulse
- 1/2 avocado
- 2 tbsp dried tomatoes
- 1/2 tsp kelp
- 1 fresh date, pitted
- 1/4 onion
- 1 tsp apple cider vinegar
- 1 tsp tamari
- 1 tbsp olive oil

Roughly chop tomatoes, carrots and celery. Rinse the dulse.
Put everything in the blender and blend till smooth. That's it!
Perfect sauce for every occasion.

■ ■ ■ ■ It is often asserted that the lycopene in tomatoes is only
bioavailable when cooked. This is not strictly accurate, as
although it is true to say raw tomatoes are not a good source
of this valuable antioxidant, it can still be utilised if the
tomatoes are juiced or dried, i.e. sun-dried tomatoes.

- 15 mins
- Blender
- **Serves four as a main dish or eight as a side dish**

Pizza Peppers

- 2 portions pasta sauce (p 142)
- 4 red peppers
- 1 small head broccoli
- 90 g/3 oz spinach
- 60 g/2 oz corn
- 60 g/2 oz olives
- 60 g/2 oz pine nuts

Prepare the pasta sauce. Slice the peppers in half lengthways and remove all seeds and stems. Chop the broccoli into small bite-sized pieces, about the size of cashew nuts. Fine slice the spinach. In a mixing bowl, stir up the pasta sauce, broccoli, spinach, corn, olives and pine nuts so everything is equally distributed. Spoon into the peppers. Serve immediately, or dehydrate for a few hours to warm through and bring out the flavours.

■ ■ ■ ■ If you are making this for guests, use a mixture of yellow, red and orange peppers to make it look even more attractive.

- 15 mins
- Spiral slicer, blender
- **Serves four**

Tricolore Pasta

- 2 portions pasta sauce (p 142)
- 2 courgettes
- 3 carrots
- 1 beetroot

Prepare the pasta sauce. Top and tail the courgettes, carrots and beetroot. Peel the beetroot. If you have a spiral slicer, you can make amazing noodles with your vegetables. If you don't own one of these handy gadgets, you can make noodles just using a vegetable peeler: peel the veg down ways in long strips to make tagliatelle-like strips. Or if you're in a hurry, just grate everything in a food processor. Whatever you use, you should have three piles of vegetables - green, red and orange. Stir these into your sauce. This will keep for a few days in the fridge and the vegetables will soften and the flavours improve.

■ ■ ■ ■ The flowers from the courgette plant are a delicacy which can be eaten raw in salads, or deep fried in batter like tempura.

- 20 mins
- Spiral slicer, food processor
- **Serves two**

Gourmet Pasta

- 2 portions pasta sauce (see p 142)
- 1 carrot
- 1 courgette
- 90 g/3 oz green leaf e.g. wild garlic, rocket
- 1 avocado
- 200 g/7 oz oyster mushrooms
- 2 tbsp olives
- 60 g/2 oz dried tomatoes (see p 167)
- 60 g/2 oz cashew nuts
- 2 tbsp alfalfa sprouts

Prepare the pasta sauce. Using your spiral slicer, make vegetable ribbons with the carrots and courgette. If you don't have a spiral slicer, you can use a potato peeler instead. Top and tail the vegetables, and peel away at the flesh repeatedly – these peelings are your ribbons or 'pasta'. Put the ribbons in a large mixing bowl. Next prepare your green leaf – you may want to trim it if the leaves are big, just chop it with scissors and add it into the bowl. Cube the avocado flesh, and scoop it out into the bowl. Oyster mushrooms have a very strong flavour. Fine slice them, so they add a meaty texture to your salad, without being overpowering. Add them to the mix, along with the olives, dried tomatoes, and pasta sauce. Give it all a good stir with a spoon, to get it evenly coated. Divide the mixture between two serving bowls. Chop the nuts in the food processor, so that they are not ground, but are in pieces about the same size as grated cheese. Garnish each serving with alfalfa and a sprinkling of cashews.

■ ■ ■ ■ Wild garlic is native to England and is easy to find in the hedgerows in spring. It is a soft green leaf with a pungent garlic aroma, and you can eat the garlic-flavoured flowers too!

- 20 mins
- Blender
- **Serves two**

Chilli

- 1 large or 2 small beetroot
- 3 tomatoes
- 1 red chilli pepper, stem and seeds removed
- 4 fresh dates, pitted
- 1 tbsp apple cider vinegar
- 2 tbsp olive oil
- 1 tsp tamari
- 1/4 onion
- 2 cloves garlic
- 2 tbsp dulse flakes
- 30 g/1 oz mixed beansprouts (see p 42)

Top, tail, and peel the beetroot. If you have a high power blender, you can just cube it at this stage, in preparation. Otherwise, grate it, and set it aside. Put the tomato, chilli, dates, vinegar, olive oil, tamari, onion and garlic in the blender, and blend to a purée. Once it's smooth, add the grated beetroot and dulse flakes and stir in by hand. If you're using the high power blender, you can add the cubed beetroot and dulse, and blend it on a 3 or 4 setting – where the beetroot is half-blended, half-chunky. Add the beansprouts, and stir in by hand.

You can serve this in two ways. Add some ready-prepared veg, like sliced mushrooms, cubed peppers, broccoli florets, sweet corn kernels or shredded spinach leaves. Stir them in to make a vegetable chilli. Or leave it as it is and serve tacos. Get some little gem lettuce leaves as your taco shells. Fill each leaf with the chilli, and top with a raw mayonnaise (try Avo Mayo from *Eat Smart Eat Raw*, or Cashew Cream Cheese (p 67) and some alfalfa sprouts.

■ ■ ■ ■ Chilli peppers are thought to have been cultivated in Central and South America for more than seven thousand years.

■ Biscuits and crackers

Unfortunately, there is no way round it; you really do need a dehydrator for the recipes in this section. The cheapest and smallest ones on the market are sold through the Organic Gardening catalogue (www.organiccatalog.com), and are a good buy if you are just dabbling. However, if you think you are serious about raw foods, the only option is the Excalibur 9-Tray (from www.detoxyourworld.com). Nine trays may seem a lot, but dehydrating usually involves bulk quantities, and you will be amazed at how quickly you can fill it up. They come in black and white and are about the size of a microwave oven. When they're on (usually for 12-24 hr periods) they emit a low humming sound, caused by the fan at the back of the machine. They also tend to fill the house with lovely home-baking smells – anything with cinnamon or onion in is particularly pungent. I think they're set to be the latest trend. A few years ago, juicing was just for the health freaks, now every home has one. In the same way, I think people are going to start cottoning on to what fun you can have with a dehydrator, and they'll soon become the latest must-have kitchen accessory.

It is perfectly possible to be raw without a dehydrator. I was raw six years before I got one. Purists argue that dehydrated food shouldn't be classed as raw anyhow, and it's certainly true that you shouldn't eat too much of it. But if you want raw biscuits it really is indispensable.

- 15 mins, soaking 8–12 hrs, drying 18 hrs
- Blender and dehydrator
- **Makes about 30 crackers**

■ Crunchy Quinoa Crackers

Quinoa (pronounced keen-wah) is an ancient Aztec grain. It is a complete protein, and one of the few grains that is not glutinous in its cooked form. It is tricky to sprout, but if you get a good batch, it is a lovely light addition to salads.

- 120 g/4 oz quinoa, sprouted (p 42)
- 60 g/2 oz flax seeds, soaked overnight (see below)
- 1 tsp tamari
- 2 tbsp olive oil
- 2 tbsp nori flakes

Sprout the quinoa a couple of days in advance. Soak the flax seeds overnight in 250 ml/8 fl oz water. They will form a gloopy mass. Spoon it into the blender, along with the tamari and olive oil, and blend until you have a cream and you can't see any seeds left. Stir in the quinoa grains and nori flakes by hand. Spread onto two dehydrator trays and dry for 12 hrs. Slice, turn, and dehydrate for a further 6 hours.

■ ■ ■ ■ You can also eat quinoa leaves, which are similar to spinach and chard as they are from the same family.

- Grinder, food processor, dehydrator
- 10 mins
- **Makes 12**

■ Oatcakes

Although oats are glutinous, like wheat, people are much less likely to have a problem with digesting them than they are with wheat. If you buy raw oat groats and sprout them, then the starches turn to sugars and the gluten content becomes negligible. However, in this recipe they haven't been sprouted, so best not to eat too many. But they really capture that crumbly wholesome feel of traditional oatcakes; one or two spread with tahini or jam (p 221) make a lovely snack.

- 150 g/5 oz oat groats, ground into flour
- 2 tbsp olive oil
- 1/4 tsp sea salt
- 125 ml/4 fl oz water

Grind your oats into flour using a coffee grinder or high power blender. You can mix this lot up by hand or in a food processor. Using a teaspoon, spoon the mix onto a dehydrator tray, flattening out each spoonful into a round about 7 cm/3 in in diameter – best not to try it in sheets, it's very crumbly. Also, don't make them too thin or they will crumble when you try and turn them over. Dry for 10 hrs, then flip them over with a spatula, and do them for a couple more hours on the other side.

■ ■ ■ ■ Oats are a staple food in Scotland, whereas in England until relatively recently they were considered to be only good enough for animal feed. The English had a saying which went, "Oats are only fit to be fed to horses and Scotsmen"; the Scottish reply was, "And England has the finest horses, while Scotland has the finest men."

- 15 mins and sprouting 3 days, soaking 4 hrs and dehydrating 24 hrs
- Juicer with blank plate, dehydrator
- **Serves eight**

■ Miso Bread

Essene bread is one of the few things that does work in an oven if you don't have access to a dehydrator. Switch your oven to the lowest temperature, and leave the bread in for 12-24 hrs. It's heated too much to be considered raw this way, but it's still great bread.

- 2 tbsp pumpkin seeds
- 2 tbsp sunflower seeds
- 2 tbsp sesame seeds
- 2 tbsp hemp seeds
- 1/2 onion
- 180 g/6 oz wheat, sprouted (p 42)
- 1 tsp miso

Sprout the wheat three days in advance. You need a gear juicer (as opposed to a centrifugal juicer) for this recipe, to really purée the ingredients. Soak all the seeds for two to four hours, then rinse and drain. Push them through your juicer with the blank plate on, they should go through easily because they've been soaked. Then push the onion through, and then all the wheat. Add the miso into the bowl, and mix in with your hands, kneading all the ingredients together like dough, making sure the seeds are evenly mixed in. On a dehydrator tray, shape into a loaf shape about 4 cm/2 in high and dry for 18 hrs. Turn, and dry for another 6 hrs. Serve with soup or a salad (it goes well with rocket).

■ ■ ■ ■ If you want to avoid wheat, even in its sprouted form, you can substitute kamut or spelt in this recipe, which are ancient grains very similar to wheat.

- 10 mins, 24 hrs dehydrating
- Juicer, dehydrator
- **Makes one loaf**

■ Rye Bread

Rye bread has a distinctive, interesting flavour. When grains are sprouted, the starches are turned into sugars, so sprouted breads are suitable for people who have gluten intolerance.

- 330 g/11 oz rye grain, sprouted (p 42)
- 4 tbsp olive oil
- 1 tbsp Seagreens (p 48)
- 2 tbsp nutritional yeast flakes
- 1 tbsp tamari

Sprout the rye grain for three days. Using a heavy duty juicer, push the grain through with the blank plate on. Transfer to a mixing bowl, and add the remaining ingredients, kneading with your hands until they are thoroughly mixed. On a dehydrator tray, shape the dough into a loaf about 3 cm/1½ in high. Dry for 12 hrs, then flip over, and dry for a further 6-12 hrs, until crusty. Serve spread with tahini and topped with alfalfa sprouts. Lovely with a green salad like Simple Salad (p 102).

■ ■ ■ ■ Rye is one of the more recently cultivated grains, originating as an agricultural crop in Germany around two thousand years ago, and today is mostly grown in Russia.

- 15 mins and pre-soaking 8-12 hrs and dehydrating 18 hrs
- Blender, dehydrator
- Makes about 40 crackers

Lebanese Cauliflower Crackers

These make a deliciously light, wholesome cracker. Zaatar is a traditional Lebanese flavouring, which you can find in any speciality grocers. It is a blend of thyme, sumac and sesame seeds.

- 150 g/5 oz Brazil nuts
- 60 g/2 oz flax seeds
- 1 medium cauliflower
- 2 lemons
- 2 tbsp zaatar

Soak the Brazil nuts and flax seeds overnight in 500 ml (16 fl oz) water. They will swell and absorb all the water. Roughly chop the cauliflower (you can use the leaves for juicing, they're very nutritious). Juice the lemons. Put the nuts, seeds, cauliflower and lemon juice in the blender and blend to a thick cream. Stir in the zaatar by hand, making sure it's mixed right through to the bottom. You can actually eat it like this, I like the taste, and the flax seeds are very beneficial when eaten this way. You could have some with a salad and eat it with a spoon. But if you're making crackers, spread it as thin as it will go on a dehydrator tray, in one big square. It should cover two trays. After about 12 hrs, score through the biscuits into squares, you should be able to get about 20 out of each tray. Dehydrate for about another 6 hrs, until they're really crispy. These are so tasty and flavoursome, you can eat them as they are – they make good snacks.

■ ■ ■ ■ You can make these crackers with other vegetables too. Try making courgette crackers by substituting 500 g/1 lb courgettes for the cauliflower, and omit the lemon juice.

- 5 mins, 8–12 hrs soaking, 18 hrs drying
- Blender, dehydrator
- **Makes 20**

■ Tomato Crackers

This is a gorgeous, tangy biscuit, bursting with flavour.

- 150 g/5 oz flax seeds, soaked 8-12 hrs in 500 ml (16 fl oz) water
- 6 tomatoes, quartered
- 60 g/2 oz dried tomatoes
- 1 lemon, juiced
- 1 tbsp tamari
- 4 cloves garlic
- 15 g/$\frac{1}{2}$ oz Atlantic sea salad

Pre-soak your flax seeds. Pour all the ingredients, bar the dulse flakes, in the blender, and blend until the flax seeds and tomato are amalgamated into a beautiful pink mixture. Stir in the dulse flakes by hand. Spread onto two drying trays, and dry for 12 hrs. Score each sheet into four by five crackers, and flip them over. Dry for a further 6 hrs, until crisp. Stored in an airtight container, will keep for up to a week.

■ ■ ■ ■ There are over a thousand varieties of tomato. They come in a huge range of sizes and colours, including yellow, orange, green, purple and brown.

- 30 mins and pre-soaking 8-12 hrs and dehydrating 18 hrs
- Blender, dehydrator
- **40 biscuits**

■ Traffic Light Biscuits

These are a great way to get more vegetables into children, they love playing with the different colour biscuits and making patterns on their plates. Just make sure they don't eat all the red ones and leave all the spinach ones!

- 150 g/5 oz Brazil nuts
- 60 g/2 oz flax seeds

Add one of the following vegetables:
- To make red biscuits, add three red peppers
- To make amber biscuits, add two large carrots
- To make green biscuits, add 250 g/8 oz spinach.
- Water to blend

Pre-soak the Brazil nuts and flax seeds in 500 ml (16 fl oz) water. Put the nuts, seeds and whichever veg you are blending in the blender (if you are not using a Vitamix you may want to grind the nuts and seeds first, for ease of blending). The red pepper biscuits shouldn't need any water, the carrot mix definitely will, and the spinach just a little.

Using a teaspoon, make small circles of the mix on the dehydrator tray – only about 3 cm/1¹/₂ in diameter, the right size for fitting three on a plate, in a vertical row. If you want to make proper traffic lights, then you need to make three batches of biscuits - pepper for red, carrot for amber, and spinach for green.

Dehydrate for 12–18 hrs until slightly crispy. Each batch makes at least 40 little biscuits. They will keep for weeks in an airtight container.

■ ■ ■ ■ Brazil nuts are not farmed, but only grow wild in the Amazon rainforest. Because the rainforests are being cut down, there are actually fewer and fewer Brazil nuts available in the global marketplace, while demand for this healthy food increases, which is why the price of Brazils has risen so much over the past decade.

- ■ 5 mins, dehydrating
- ■ Blender, dehydrator
- ■ **Makes 30 crackers**

■ Olive Crackers

These are gorgeous, rich, substantial, healthy – the perfect between meal snack, or accompaniment to salads.

- ■ 200 g/7 oz pitted olives
- ■ 1/2 onion, peeled and chopped
- ■ 330 g/11 oz rye, sprouted (p 42)
- ■ 60 g/2 oz flax seeds, ground

Sprout your rye grain for three days. Grind your flax seeds. Put everything in the blender and blend to a cream. Spread thin on to a couple of dehydrator trays and dry for 12 hrs. Score into crackers, about 16 to each sheet, turn and dry for another 4-6 hrs. Store in an airtight container for up to two weeks.

■ ■ ■ ■ Olives are one of the most ancient foods known; they play an important role in Greek mythology, and are mentioned frequently in the Bible.

- 10 mins, sprouting, dehydrating 18 hrs
- Blender, dehydrator
- **Makes 40 biscuits**

Spelt and Coriander Biscuits

Spelt is an ancient form of wheat, popular with people who have wheat intolerance. It is very similar to wheat, with a delightful nutty flavour. These make a very tasty wholesome snack.

- 250 g/8 oz spelt grain, sprouted (p 42)
- 60 g/2 oz flax seeds, ground
- 1 onion
- Small bunch coriander
- 2 tbsp olive oil
- 1 tbsp tamari
- 250 ml/8 fl oz water

Sprout the spelt for three days. Grind the flax seed. Peel and chop the onion; loosely chop the coriander. Put everything together in the blender and blend to a thick purée. Spread onto two drying trays, fairly thin. Dry for 12 hrs. Score each sheet into five by four squares, and flip them over. Dry for a further six hours. Store in an airtight container; they will keep for a couple of weeks.

■ ■ ■ ■ Although cultivated for around 7,000 years, spelt fell out of favour probably because it is tougher than wheat and so harder to process. It has been made more popular in recent years as people look for wheat alternatives.

- 5 mins, soaking 8-12 hrs, dehydrating 12 hrs
- Blender, dehydrator
- **Makes about 30 biscuits**

Sand Biscuits

My son named these, because they look like sand, and they taste of the seaside too, with the kelp and sea salad in. And of course, you can put two together and make a sandwich!

- 150 g/5 oz Brazil nuts, soaked 8-12 hrs
- 60 g/2 oz flax seeds, ground
- 1 tbsp miso
- 1 tsp kelp powder
- 500 ml/16 fl oz water
- 4 tbsp Atlantic sea salad

Pre-soak your Brazil nuts the day before. Put all the ingredients apart from the sea salad in a blender, and blend for a few minutes until it has thickened (you may need to add more water). Stir in the sea salad by hand, making sure it's evenly distributed throughout the mixture. Shape into flat biscuits about 5 cm/2 in across and dehydrate for about 12 hrs.

■ ■ ■ ■ Brazil nuts are the richest natural source of selenium, a mineral that is particularly important for men's health and has been linked with the prevention of prostate cancer.

- 5 mins, soaking 8-12 hrs, dehydrating 12 hrs
- Blender, dehydrator
- **Makes 30 biscuits**

■ Lisa's Raw Indian Bars

This is based on a recipe my wonderful friend Lisa Gylsen sent to me. The flavour is a bit strong for children, but very popular with adults.

- 200 g/7 oz cashews, soaked 8-12 hrs
- 1 red onion
- 120 g/4 oz fresh coconut
- 1 clove garlic
- 2 lime leaves
- 1 tsp miso
- 1 tbsp curry powder
- 1 tsp cinnamon
- 4 lemons, juiced

Soak the cashews overnight. Peel and chop the onion. Chop the coconut into small pieces to make it easy for your blender to break down. Put everything in the blender and keep mashing until there are no lumps of coconut left or stray bits of lime leaf. Spread the mixture on drying trays and dehydrate for 12 hrs. Score into rectangles about 10 cm/4 in long and 5 cm/2 in wide. Store in an airtight container in the fridge.

■ ■ ■ ■ Lime leaves come from a wild lime tree, and are also known as kaffir lime leaves. They are usually sold dried, or frozen.

■ Extras

More reasons to get a dehydrator. None of these are essentials, but they are all things I keep a stock of to liven up a salad, and add a bit of bite and crunch. They make good snacks too – just a handful or two will fill a gap between meals and provide a nourishing and sustaining burst of energy. They're quick and easy to make, and really worth trying. It's the little touches like these that can help you stay raw by adding a bit of variety and preventing you from getting into a rut with your food.

I haven't put serving sizes for any of these recipes because it's impossible to say how much you'll get through: some people will want to make a batch and keep them in the cupboard for a month, using them sparingly as a salad garnish say, others will sit down and eat the whole recipe in one or two sittings just as they are.

- 10 mins and dehydrating 12 hrs
- Blender, dehydrator

■ Broccoli Bits

Broccoli is one of my favourite foods. It's so full of nutrients; it's practically a superfood in its own right. When I was breastfeeding Zachary, I couldn't get enough of it; I'd drink half a pint of broccoli juice every day. So I thought I'd try drying it and seeing what I came up with. Well, I hit the jackpot. These little nibbles are so tasty, and best of all the boys eat loads. If you have a child who is fussy about their greens, this is a marvellous way to get some of that tip top nutrition in them.

- 2 kg/4 lb broccoli
- 1 onion, peeled and chopped
- 4 lemons, juiced
- 125 ml/4 fl oz olive oil

Put the broccoli, onion, lemon juice and olive oil in the blender and blend to a purée. You can add more olive oil if you need to, or just if you want them to turn out richer. Spread on a dehydrator sheet and dry for 12 hrs. When it's done, just break pieces off the tray, they'll crumble into chunks. Store them in an airtight container. You can snack on them as they are, like crisps, or sprinkle them on salads. The lemon juice makes them wonderfully tangy.

■ ■ ■ ■ The name broccoli comes from the Italian and means 'cabbage sprout'.

- 5 mins and dehydrating 12 hrs
- Grater, dehydrator

Carrot Crunch

We used to always have Bombay mix in the cupboard to add to our salads for a bit of crunch. It was one of the last cooked foods to go in our house. Now I have this instead.

- 500 g/1 lb carrots
- 3 tbsp olive oil
- 2 tbsp garam masala
- 2 tbsp poppy seeds
- 2 tbsp sesame seeds

Top and tail the carrots, and grate them finely. In a bowl, mix all the ingredients together, so that the seeds coat the carrots. Be careful not to use too much oil or they will not go crispy. Spread onto dehydrator trays (it should cover two trays), and dry for 12 hrs. Store in an airtight container.

■ ■ ■ ■ Carrots are recognised to be one of the best dietary sources of vitamin A. 100 g /3 oz carrots contains about six times the RDA of this important vitamin.

- 5 mins and dehydrating 12 hrs
- Dehydrator
- **Makes about 500 g/1 lb crunch**

Curry Crunch

Like the previous recipe, this evolved as a replacement for Bombay mix. It's so yummy; you can just eat a handful or two as a snack.

- 300 g/10 oz buckwheat, sprouted
- 2 tbsp curry powder
- 2 tbsp sesame oil

Sprout the buckwheat for around two days so it has a little tail. In a bowl, mix it with the curry powder and sesame oil so the sprouts are evenly coated. Spread on to your dehydrator trays and dry for 12 hrs. Stored in an airtight tub, these will keep for a good few weeks.

■ ■ ■ ■ Dehydrated buckwheat makes great flour for raw pastries and cakes: just sprout, dehydrate, and grind and use instead of oats or nuts in any recipe.

- 5 mins and drying 18 hrs
- Blender, dehydrator

Nori Crisps

In *Eat Smart Eat Raw* there is a recipe for tomato crisps, which are a staple in our kitchen. But as tomatoes are very acidic, I wasn't too happy about the boys having a lot of them. So I developed this recipe instead. Cucumbers are very alkaline and cleansing.

- 500 g/1 lb tomatoes
- 500 g/1 lb cucumbers
- 2 tbsp nori flakes

Blend the tomatoes and cucumbers together to a liquid. Then briefly whiz in the nori flakes so they're evenly distributed throughout the mixture. Spread onto dehydrator trays (makes about four trays). Dry for 18 hrs. Snap into pieces; how big you want them is up to you. Store in an airtight container and keep for up to a month.

■ ■ ■ ■ You can make just cucumber crisps by blending up cucumbers on their own, but they're not as tasty and the sheets turn out paper thin because cucumber is so watery.

- 5 mins and 12 hrs dehydrating
- Fine slicer, dehydrator

Sweet Potato Crisps

I've tried turning every vegetable you can think of into crisps – beetroot, parsnip, carrot, and more. The trick is to slice them as thinly as possible; you need a machine with a really fine blade. But even then, most of them turn out woody and not that crispy – not great. The only two that work really well for me are sweet potato and courgette. You can use any sort of spice you want on them – there's a really good range made by Seasoned Pioneers which make authentic gourmet crisps.

- 1 large sweet potato
- 1 tbsp olive oil
- 1 tbsp curry powder

I usually don't bother peeling the sweet potato for this, just wash it. Slice it either with a mandolin or the fine blade on your food processor. Transfer it to a bowl, and mix in the oil and curry powder so the pieces of potato are evenly coated and none of them are sticking together. Don't use too much oil or they won't go crispy. Spread them evenly on your dehydrating trays – it doesn't matter if they overlap a bit, just as long as they're not all heaped on top of each other. Dry for 12 hrs then store in an airtight container. They only stay crispy for a day or two, which is why I haven't given a very large amount – you need to eat them all straight away.

■ ■ ■ ■ Never mind the fancy packs of fried root vegetable crisps which cost a fortune – these are just as good and cost pennies.

- 5 mins and 12 hrs dehydrating
- Fine slicer, dehydrator

Courgette Crisps

These are my favourites. Light and tasty, we often have a handful each with tea.

- 500 g/1 lb courgettes
- 1 tbsp sesame oil
- 2 tbsp Chinese 5 spice

Top and tail the courgettes. Using a mandolin or the fine slicing plate on your food processor, slice them up. Then transfer them to a mixing bowl and coat them evenly with the oil and spice. Spread on the dehydrator trays and dry for 12 hrs. Store in an airtight container and eat within a day or two.

■ ■ ■ ■ These are perfect with guacamole (p 54) or Coriander Chutney (p 61).

- 5 mins, 12 hrs dehydrating
- Dehydrator
- **Serves 4**

■ Dulse Crisps

You can hardly get more nutritious than dulse. Clearspring, the biggest UK retailers of Japanese foods, recommend deep frying it for a gorgeous snack. Obviously, we don't go in for that, so here are raw crisps. Surprisingly tasty, and unlike their deep-fried alternative, no guilt involved.

- 1 packet dulse
- 1 tbsp olive oil

Rinse the dulse and separate the strands. Put it in a bowl and lightly coat with the olive oil. Spread onto drying trays and dry for 12 hrs. You don't need any salt as sea vegetables are naturally salty. You can also try this with wakame, although it needs soaking for about 10 mins first. Best eaten straight away, but you can probably get away with storing them in an airtight container for a few days.

■ ■ ■ ■ Sea vegetables are not just an important part of Japanese cuisine. In fact, they are enjoyed by most countries with extensive coastal regions such as Ireland, Iceland, France, Australia, and Hawaii.

- 10 mins, 24 hrs drying
- Dehydrator
- **Makes enough for four**

Dried Tomatoes

People were always asking me if you could make sun-dried tomatoes in the dehydrator, and I could never figure out a way of doing it. If you slice them in a food processor, you lose a lot of the juice and seeds, and they come out too thin and chewy. If you cut them in half, like the shop-bought ones, they just take forever to do, and never fully dry out. It took me a long while to discover that you could just slice them thickly, and get that meaty effect you get in the sun-dried ones.

- 16 tomatoes

Slice each tomato into slices of 1–2 cm/$^1/_2$-1 in thick. I usually find I get about 4 slices out of each tomato. You can use beef tomatoes, and get more slices, or cherry tomatoes simply halved work well. Arrange them on a drying tray – you should get about 8 tomatoes to a tray.

Dry for 24 hrs – some fatter and end pieces might take even longer. Store in an airtight container and eat within a couple of days.

■ ■ ■ ■ If you like the oily effect you get from shop-bought jars of tomatoes, you can store your home-made ones in jars of olive oil with a few leaves of basil and a couple of cloves of garlic. Marinade for at least a day, and add to salads.

- 2 mins
- **Serves one**

Zachary's Snack

This couldn't be simpler, and makes a wonderful nibble. I've given a basic amount – you can multiply it up to feed a family or even a party. Good for school lunches instead of crisps.

- 1 tbsp broccoli bits (see p 160)
- 1 tbsp sunflower and pumpkin seeds (see below)
- 1 tbsp dulse flakes
- 1 tbsp lentil or mung sprouts

Crumble the broccoli bits so they're the same size as the seeds. It's always best to soak seeds first to activate the enzymes - if you want to give them a crunch back, soak them then dehydrate them for a bit. Mix the lot together and munch, for the most nutritious snack you're ever going to come across. Doesn't really store well; the bits start to go soggy. Best to make only as much as you need, and eat it straight away.

■ ■ ■ ■ This is great made with Raw Living 'Sunseeds', which is a mix of sunflower and pumpkin seeds ready sprouted, marinated in tamari and dehydrated.

- 5 mins, 4-8hrs soaking
- Dehydrator
- **Serves two**

Cereal

For a long time, we had fruit for breakfast, either a pudding or a smoothie. But as we detoxified, we noticed more and more the effect this early morning sugar hit had on our bodies, and began to search for an alternative. This (or raw porridge) is what the boys have for their breakfast most mornings.

- 30 g/1 oz raisins
- 30 g/1 oz pumpkin or sunflower seeds
- 120 g/4 oz buckwheat bits (see below)
- 1 tsp agave syrup
- 1 tbsp flax oil
- 1 tsp lecithin granules

Soak the raisins and seeds for at least four hours. We put ours in to soak just before we go to bed, ready for the morning. Drain them, and put them in a mixing bowl with all the other ingredients. Give them a good stir round, so the agave and oil are evenly coating the cereal. Divide into two bowls and serve.

Variations:
- You can substitute just about any dried fruit, nuts or seeds in this that you like.
- You can substitute tahini or nut butter for the oil.
- You can add 1 tbsp carob powder for carob cereal.
- On special occasions you can add 2 tbsp cacao nibs and 2 tbsp goji berries for a superfood cereal!

■ ■ ■ ■ To make the buckwheat bits, sprout some buckwheat groats for about three days, and then dry them in the dehydrator for 12 hrs. 300 g/10 oz unsoaked buckwheat will make about 450 g/15 oz of crunchy bits (or six servings of cereal). Store in an airtight container, and they will keep for a couple of months.

■ 5 mins

■ Quickles

Pickles for cheats! I've tried to make sauerkraut a handful of times, but it's yet to work, and there are a few good raw ones available (like Biona and Bionova), so it doesn't seem worth the bother. But these are so easy, and surprisingly good.

- ■ 1/2 cucumber
- ■ 250 ml/8 fl oz apple cider vinegar

or

- ■ 2 onions
- ■ 250 ml/8 fl oz apple cider vinegar

Chop the cucumber or onion into small chunks. Put in a jar of vinegar and store in the fridge. Eat the next day (will keep for a few weeks). It's that easy.

■ ■ ■ ■ I use the vinegar that's left when we've finished a jar of gherkins (Biona use organic apple cider vinegar). You can usually use it twice before you have to throw it out.

- 10 mins, 12 hrs dehydrating
- Food processor, dehydrator
- **Serves four**

Plantain Chips

Plantains are a staple food in many parts of Africa and Asia, and can often be picked up very cheaply in markets. Green plantain is usually used in savoury dishes; yellow plantain is ripe, and more like bananas. Green plantains work better for crisp making as they are firmer and go crunchier.

- 3 plantains
- 2 tbsp olive oil

Fine slice the plantain in a food processor or salad slicer. Transfer them in a bowl and coat them in oil – add a little chilli powder if you like a bit of heat. Arrange them over two drying trays, separating them out as much as possible. Dry for 12 hrs. Store in an airtight container, and eat as soon as possible – they won't go off quickly, but they will soften and lose their crunch.

■ ■ ■ ■ Traidcraft do some lovely fairly-traded plantain chips, which aren't raw, but they're fried in coconut oil, so they're a much healthier alternative to potato crisps.

■ Puddings

Everyone knows the saying 'you can't have your cake and eat it'. Well with raw foods that is just not true. I'm here to tell you that this is a pudding revolution! Raw desserts taste amazing - they can be just as fat-laden and syrupy sweet as your heart desires. But because we are using healthy fats that the body loves, and nutritious sweeteners that don't destabilise blood sugar levels, you can eat as much of them as you like. In fact, some of them are so good you can eat them for breakfast lunch and dinner and feel super-energised! I have a passion for puddings – it gives me great joy to feed pudding to people at every possible opportunity.

- 15 mins, 4-8 hrs soaking
- Blender
- **Serves four**

Carob Coconut Pudding

It's just a guess, but I think you could probably live on this, it contains so much nutrition. Hemp seeds are one of my favourite foods; they contain nearly everything the body needs to live on. Whole hemp seeds haven't been processed so they are a better source of nutrition but the shells have quite a strong taste and crunchy texture which some people find unpalatable. For this reason, hulled seeds are very popular, as they have a lovely creamy taste. You can use whichever you prefer in this recipe.

- 4 bananas, peeled and chopped
- 120 g/4 oz fresh dates, pitted
- 60 g/2 oz carob powder
- 2 lemons, juiced
- 250 ml/8 fl oz water
- 60 g/2 oz hemp seeds, soaked 4-8 hrs,
- 1 fresh coconut (see p 77)

Put the bananas, dates, carob powder, lemon juice and water in the blender, and blend to a liquid. Then add the hemp seeds and coconut pieces, and blend for a few minutes until you have a cream. If you haven't got a high-powered blender, you may need to grate the coconut in the food processor first, to make it easier for your machine. Serve within 24 hrs and store in the fridge; fresh coconut doesn't keep well.

■ ■ ■ ■ Banana plants are part of the same family as lilies and orchids.

- 5 mins, soaking 8-12 hrs
- Blender
- **Serves two**

■ Breakfast Pudding

A light but filling breakfast to set you up for the day. The flax oil and lecithin give the pudding a real creaminess, as well as being a valuable source of nutrition. Lecithin helps with the absorption of fats so you can get the most out of those all-important essential fatty acids in the flax oil.

- 2 apples
- 1 banana
- 60 g/2 oz sesame seeds, soaked 8-12 hrs
- 30 g/1 oz raisins, soaked 8-12 hrs
- 1 tbsp flax oil
- 1 tbsp lecithin granules

Soak your sesame seeds and raisins overnight. Prepare the apples and banana for the blender by removing skins, stems, seeds etc. Pop all your ingredients in the blender and whiz up to a smooth purée. Best eaten the same day.

■ ■ ■ ■ If you've got any leftovers, you can spread the mixture onto a dehydrator sheet, and dry it until it turns into a chewy snack.

- 10 mins, 2 hrs soaking
- Blender
- **Serves two**

Gorgeous Goji Pudding

Wow! This bright orange pudding is sure to give you a lift. Goji berries are a superfood, the most nutrient dense fruit on the planet.

- 60 g/2 oz goji berries, soaked 2 hrs
- 1 avocado
- 1 banana
- 1 medjool date, pitted
- 1 tbsp agave nectar

Soak the gojis in just enough water to cover them. When they've plumped up, drink the soaking water, it's yummy. Slice the avocado in half, remove the stone, and using a spoon, scoop the flesh out into the blender. Put the berries in the blender along with the banana, peeled and broken into chunks, the date, and the agave. Blend to a cream. If your blender isn't strong enough, add a little water, until it will keep going. Best eaten the same day.

■ ■ ■ ■ Goji berries were the health heroes of 2006 – suddenly they were everywhere, in mueslis, trail mixes, and snack bars. They are very common in Chinese cuisine, where they have been eaten for thousands of years, and are also used medicinally.

- 5 mins
- Blender
- **Serves two**

■ Best Ever Chocolate Pudding

This is probably one of the most popular raw food desserts. If you're new to raw foods, you'll be amazed at how avocado can form the base for one of the most luscious raw puddings around. If you're an experienced raw fooder, you've probably had chocolate pudding many times. It's my favourite sweet treat, and so easy to prepare – ready in minutes, with no pre-soaking or dehydrating necessary.

- 30 g/1 oz cacao nibs, ground
- 1 large avocado
- 1 banana
- 1 medjool date
- 1 tbsp agave nectar
- 1 tbsp hemp oil
- 30 g/1 oz carob powder

Grind your cacao in a coffee grinder or high power blender. Slice the avocado in half, remove the pit, and scoop out the flesh with a spoon, straight into the blender. Peel the banana, break into quarters, and add to the blender. Remove the stone from the date and pop it in the jug too. Add the remaining ingredients. If you haven't got cacao, you can use double carob powder instead; it won't give you the same chocolate hit, but it will taste nearly as divine. Turn the blender on, and start whizzing. If your blender is having difficulties, you can add some water until it starts turning over. Keep it turning for a minute to make sure it's really smooth and creamy. Spoon out into two serving bowls; decorate with carob chips or goji berries if you fancy. Or add a tablespoon of maca powder for a lover's pudding.

■ ■ ■ ■ Cacao, the raw chocolate bean, is causing a revolution in the raw food world and beyond. Everyone loves the chocolate that loves you back!

- 5 mins, 8-12 hrs soaking
- Blender
- **Serves four**

Toffee Cream

This is a rich gooey dessert that goes brilliantly with fresh berries in the summer or sliced apples and pears in the autumn.

- 200 g/7 oz cashews, soaked 8-12 hrs
- 60 g/2 oz carob powder
- 4 tbsp olive oil
- 2 tbsp agave nectar
- 250 ml/8 fl oz water

Soak your cashews in advance. Put all the ingredients together in a blender and blend to a smooth purée. Will keep in the fridge for about four days.

■ ■ ■ ■ Instead of cashews, you can substitute hulled hemp seeds, macadamias or pine nuts if you prefer.

- 5 mins, freezing 12 hrs, pre-soaking 1 hr
- Blender
- **Serves two**

Can't Beta It

Apricots and goji berries are both excellent sources of beta carotene (vitamin A). This is a beautiful bright and breezy summery pudding.

- 2 bananas, frozen 12 hrs
- 60 g/2 oz gojis, soaked 1 hr
- 8 fresh apricots

Peel your bananas, break them into small chunks, and put them in a bag or tub in the freezer for at least 12 hrs. It isn't essential to use frozen bananas, but you get a much thicker pudding if you do.
Soak the gojis for about an hour and then drain (drink the soak water, its gorgeous.). Remove the stones from the apricots, and put the flesh in the blender along with the gojis and bananas. Blend until there are no chunks of banana left. Serve immediately.

■ ■ ■ ■ A single apricot contains about 20% of the RDA for vitamin A, so this pudding should easily satisfy your daily requirement.

- 5 mins, soaking 8-12 hrs, freezing 20 mins
- Ice cream maker, blender
- **Serves four**

■ Hemp Ice Cream

You need an ice cream maker for these ice cream recipes, but it is so worth the investment for an amazing variety of raw ice creams. Once you have tried them, you will be hooked – we have them every week throughout the summer. I have a Magimix, and it is so quick and easy to use.

- 250 g/8 oz whole hemp seeds, soaked 8-12 hrs
- 500 ml/16 fl oz water
- 120 g/4 oz fresh dates
- 4 tbsp olive oil

Pre-soak the hemp seeds. Blend everything to a cream. Pour into the ice cream maker, and proceed according to the manufacturer's instructions. You should get fantastic results in less than half an hour.

■ ■ ■ ■ **Variation:** replace the hemp seeds with pumpkin seeds for a green ice cream.

- 5 mins, soaking 8-12 hrs, freezing 20 mins
- Ice cream maker, blender
- **Serves four**

■ Halva Ice Cream

We love halva. We used to be addicted to vegan halva made with grape juice, but it's not raw, and too much of those cooked sesame seeds aren't health-giving and start to clog you up. This, on the other hand, is guilt-free!

- 400 g/14 oz sesame seeds, soaked 8-12 hrs
- 120 g/4 oz fresh dates, pitted
- 500 ml/16 fl oz water
- 1 vanilla pod
- 120 g/4 oz raisins

Soak your sesame seeds in advance. Blend the sesame seeds, dates, water and vanilla to a thick cream, so there are no seedy bits or fragments of pod left. Stir in the raisins by hand. Pour into your ice cream maker, and proceed according to the manufacturer's instructions. It usually takes about 20 mins to make heavenly raw ice cream.

■ ■ ■ ■ Apparently, there is a Greek saying, *Ante re halva*! which translates as 'Get lost, halva!' and is used to offend someone by implying they are effeminate.

- 5 mins, soaking 8-12 hrs, freezing about 20 mins
- Ice cream maker, blender
- **Serves six**

Carob Ice Cream

If you can track down some lucuma powder, replace it with the carob in this recipe. Lucuma is a Peruvian fruit which has a beautiful biscuity flavour, and is Peru's most popular choice for adding to ice cream.

- 250 g/8 oz sunflower seeds, soaked 8-12 hrs
- 4 tbsp olive oil
- 90 g/3 oz carob powder
- 120 g/4 oz fresh dates, pitted
- 750 ml/27 fl oz water
- 1 tbsp cinnamon

Soak your sunflower seeds in advance. Blend everything together for a few minutes to a runny cream. Pour into your ice cream maker, and proceed according to the manufacturer's instructions. Serve with strawberries on a hot summer's day.

■ ■ ■ ■ The tallest recorded sunflower grew to 12 m or 40 ft. Sunflowers are heliotropic, i.e. as the sun moves across the sky in a day, the flower head turns to face the sun and follows it from east to west.

■ Fruit Kebabs

These are great for children to make and enjoy, although they will need supervision. Smaller children will be happy with cocktail sticks; if you are making them for older children (or adults), barbecue skewers may be preferable. Serve with a chocolate sauce or nut cream for dipping like a fondue.

- ■ Selection of firm fresh fruits, e.g. apple, pear, mango, pineapple, grapes
- ■ Selection of dried fruits, e.g. Lexia raisins, dates, apricots

I haven't given quantities as it really depends on your tastes and imagination. Gather together a selection of your favourite fruits and dried fruits; three different fruits and two different dried fruits works well. Prepare them so that you have cubes, about the size of a grape, ready to pierce on your skewer or cocktail stick. Grapes you can leave whole. Lexia raisins are extra large raisins; you can leave these whole too. Dates or apricots can be halved.
Once your fruit is ready, you can call the children to come and help you. They love choosing for themselves what to put on each stick.
It's best to have a lot more fresh fruit on than dried fruit to avoid a sugar overload. Arrange the sticks on a plate or serving dish.

■ ■ ■ ■ For parties, cut a galia melon in half, and skewer the kebabs into the skin to make a hedgehog!

- 30 mins, soaking 4-8 hrs
- Blender
- **Serves four**

Easter Apples

This is my raw approximation of crème eggs. How will you eat yours?

- 120 g/4 oz sesame seeds, soaked 4-8 hrs
- 4 small apples, e.g. Coxes
- 2 bananas
- 120 g/4 oz fresh dates
- 60 g/2 oz carob powder
- 1 tbsp grain coffee
- 1 vanilla pod

Soak your sesame seeds in advance. Chop the lids off the apples, and scoop out the core. Hollow them out as if you were making Halloween pumpkins, so you're making an apple shell, ready to fill with the carob mixture. Ideally you want about 1 cm/$1/2$ in apple flesh round the edge. Put the centre flesh aside for another use. Put all the ingredients apart from the apples in the blender, and blend to a purée. Fill each apple with the mixture, and pop the lids back on. Serve immediately.

■ ■ ■ ■ **Variation:** if you have cacao nibs, you can add 50 g/2 oz and omit the grain coffee.

- 1 hr
- Food processor, blender
- **Serves eight**

■ Goji and Macadamia Mincemeat Mess

This was Jamie Oliver's idea. Eton Mess is traditionally made with strawberries, cream and meringues. He did a Christmas version with mincemeat – this is my raw version with mincemeat, cream, and clementines. It's more or less the same mincemeat recipe from *Eat Smart Eat Raw*, but with goji berries in, and the recipe for cashew cream made with macadamia nuts instead.

Mincemeat:

- 1 orange
- 1 lemon
- 360 g/12 oz grated apple
- 120 g/4 oz Lexia raisins
- 120 g/4 oz mixed vine fruit
- 120 g/4 oz goji berries
- 60 g/2 oz dates, chopped
- 1 tbsp ground cinnamon
- 1 tsp ground ginger
- Pinch ground nutmeg
- Pinch ground cloves
- 2 tbsp olive oil
- 1 tbsp agave syrup
- 1 tbsp molasses
- 1 tsp miso

Juice the lemon and the orange, and grate the rind. Using a wooden spoon, combine every ingredient together in a large bowl, so it's nice and evenly mixed.

Macadamia Cream:

- 330 g/11 oz macadamia nuts
- 120 g/4 oz dates
- 1 vanilla pod
- 2 tbsp olive oil
- 500 ml/16 fl oz water

Put everything in the blender and whiz to a thick cream.

- 4 clementines
- 1 tbsp goji berries

Peel and separate the segments, remove the pith.

To assemble:
In a large glass dish, make a bottom layer with half the mincemeat. Cover with a layer of cream, and dot with clementines. Use the remaining mincemeat for another layer, top with cream again (you don't need to use it all, it is very rich – you may find yourself with a few spoons leftover. Refrigerate it for another day or dehydrate for a sweet snack). Finish with the clementines, arranging them artfully over the top. Sprinkle with the remaining goji berries for decoration.

■ ■ ■ ■ Raisins are unique in that they are the only dried fruit not to bear the same name as the fresh fruit – do you ever hear of people snacking on dried grapes?!

- 1 hour, soaking 8-12 hrs
- Blender
- **Serves eight**

■ Trifle

A must at Christmas. This is based around four different recipes, all from Eat Smart Eat Raw, *put together in one feast of a dessert.*

Layer one: fruit in banana jelly

- 2 kiwi fruit
- 250 g/8 oz grapes, seedless
- 2 satsumas
- 1 lemon
- 2 bananas
- 1/2 tbsp psyllium husk powder

Layer two: apple pudding

- 500 g/1 lb apples
- 120 g/4 oz raisins, soaked 4-8 hrs
- 1 tsp cinnamon

Layer three: carob pudding

- 1 avocado
- 1 banana
- 60 g/2 oz fresh dates, pitted
- 1 tbsp carob powder

Layer four: cashew cream

- 120 g/4 oz cashews, soaked 8–12 hrs
- 1 tbsp olive oil
- 2 tbsp agave nectar
- 1 vanilla pod
- 4 tbsp water

Layer five: topping

- 3 pieces dried mango
- 3 pieces dried pineapple
- 1 tbsp goji berries
- 1 tbsp cacao nibs

Find a big serving dish, preferably glass or Pyrex, so you can see all the layers through it once it's done. It needs to be quite deep – the one I use is about 8 cm/3 in deep, and 22 cm/9 in diameter. To begin, prepare the fruit. Peel the kiwi; slice each into about 16 pieces. Remove the grapes from the stem; if they are large, slice them in half. Peel the satsumas and separate the segments. Put them all together in a mixing bowl. Juice the lemon, and put it in the blender with the bananas, peeled and broken up. Blend until there are no lumps of banana left, and then add the psyllium. Blend for a further minute, until the psyllium is mixed through. Pour this mixture over the fruit pieces, and stir so they are coated evenly. Spoon the mixture into the trifle dish, flattening it out on top.

Clean out the blender, ready to make the apple pudding. Chop the apples, and remove the cores. Put them in the blender and purée. Add the soaked raisins and cinnamon, and purée again. Once the raisins are completely disappeared into the mixture, it's ready. Spoon it out straight into your serving dish, covering the fruit layer completely.

Next is my favourite, the chocolate pudding. Clean the blender out once more. Peel and break the banana, scoop out the avocado flesh, and add them both to the blender with the dates and the carob. If it won't blend nicely, you can add a little water to help it along. Once it's all amalgamated, spoon it out on top of the apple layer, flattening the top off nicely.

Finally for the blender, is cashew cream. Make sure you've cleaned it properly, or the carob will turn your cream brown. Put the cashews, olive oil, agave, vanilla and water in the blender and whiz away. You may need to add more water – up to 4 tablespoons more. Keep it running for a few minutes until you have a thick but smooth cream – if it's granular, add a little more water and blend some more. Spoon it onto the carob pudding, being careful not to let any of the brown mix in to the white.

Using scissors cut the mango and pineapple pieces into tiny bits. Sprinkle them over the cream with the goji berries and cacao for a 'hundreds and thousands' effect. There you have it – a beautiful creation that tastes as good as it looks.

■ ■ ■ ■ You can make this into Knickerbocker Glory by omitting the bottom 'jelly' layer, and serving the remaining four layers heaped into tall glasses.

- 40 mins, 24 hrs for freezing, 90 mins for defrosting
- Food processor, blender
- **Serves twelve**

Christmas Iced Bombe

This one is adapted from a Waitrose recipe card. I've always loved the combination of mincemeat and ice cream, and this dish seems a perfect marriage. It's very easy to do, and keeps for ages in the freezer.

- Mincemeat recipe (p 184)
- 8 bananas

Prepare the mincemeat recipe. Peel, chop and blend the bananas to a lump-free liquid. Stir the bananas into the mincemeat in a big bowl. Line a pudding basin or large Pyrex bowl with cling film (you may need two sheets, one going up each side). Fill the basin with the mincemeat and banana mixture, and place in the freezer for 24 hrs. Remove from the freezer 90 minutes before you're ready to eat it. After an hour at room temperature, it should be defrosted enough that you can turn the bowl upside down onto a plate and it will loosen. Remove the cling film, and leave for a further 20-30 mins to soften. If there are any leftovers, slice them up, wrap them individually, and store in the freezer. Then they just need 20-30 mins defrosting time.

■ ■ ■ ■ If you don't want to use gojis, or can't get them, you can omit them and just double the amount of vine fruit.

■ Pies, tarts and cakes

I find that making cakes is just as much fun as eating them.
There's something very therapeutic about assembling all
these gorgeous ingredients with their enticing aromas and
then creating a beautiful offering that you know your friends
and family are going to love when you share it with them.
And of course, there's all that taste testing you have to do
along the way too! None of these cakes can be knocked up
in a few minutes, but they're still considerably simpler to
make than most conventional cooked cakes. The best thing
about raw cake making is you don't have to worry too much
if something goes wrong in preparation; you don't have to
concern yourself with things not rising or burning. However
it turns out, if it ends up being a little sloppy or misshapen,
it's still going to taste amazing.

- 30 mins, setting two hours
- Food processor, blender
- **Serves eight**

Lemon Tart

We were visiting my friend Emma who is a very good vegan cake-maker (and the editor of the natural parenting magazine *Juno*), and she served us some vegan lemon tart, which inspired my raw version. The carob crust makes a wonderfully rich contrast to the sharpness of the lemons.

- 200 g/7 oz almonds
- 200 g/7 oz raisins
- 2 tbsp carob powder
- 8 lemons
- 250 g/8 oz fresh dates, pitted
- 3 bananas
- 1 tbsp psyllium

Grind the almonds in a coffee grinder or high power blender. Mash the raisins in a food processor until they become a ball. Add the almonds and the carob powder to the food processor and process until they form a smooth ball together. You may need to add a drop or two of water to make it firm. Press this mixture into a 3 cm/8 in flan tin, enough to cover the base and about 2 cm/1 in up the sides. Set aside.

To make the filling, peel the lemons and remove the seeds. Put the flesh in the blender with the dates and bananas. Blend to a liquid purée. Add the psyllium and blend some more. Immediately transfer the filling into the crust. Leave to set for a few hours in the refrigerator.

■ ■ ■ ■ Did you know a single lemon provides you with 40% RDA for vitamin C?

- 30 mins, soaking 8-12 hrs, setting 2 hrs
- Food processor, blender
- **Serves twelve**

■ Banana Crème Pie

This makes a lovely treat, it's very rich so you can't eat too much of it. Bananas and tahini are such a fabulous combination, it really hits the spot.

- Pie crust (p 194)
- 4 bananas
- 1 large apple
- 120 g/4 oz fresh dates
- 120 g/4 oz tahini
- Juice 1 lemon
- 2 tsp vanilla extract
- 1 tbsp psyllium

Prepare the pie crust (or the carob crust from the lemon tart recipe on p 191 works well too). Peel the bananas, break them into quarters and put them in the blender. Chop the apple, discard the core, and put the apple pieces in the blender. Pit the dates and add them into the blender with the tahini, lemon juice, and vanilla extract. This will easily blend to a thick cream. When it's ready, pour in the psyllium and blend for a minute to make sure it's thoroughly worked in. Quickly pour it into the pie crust. Leave to set in the fridge for a couple of hours before serving.

■ ■ ■ Bananas emit a natural gas called ethylene gas, which causes fruit to ripen. That's why placing ripe bananas next to hard fruit such as pears and avocados helps them to soften quicker. And why bananas should be stored separately from other fruit like oranges and lemons, not in the fruit bowl, unless you want them to get those soft moldy white patches.

- 30 mins, soaking 8-12 hrs, setting 2 hrs
- Blender, food processor
- **Serves twelve**

■ Apple Crème Pie

Research suggests that cinnamon might improve glucose control for diabetics; half a teaspoon of cinnamon a day has produced noticeable reductions in blood sugar levels. So when you add it to your puddings not only are you improving the flavour, you could be helping to balance out your blood sugar.

- 90 g/3 oz sesame seeds, soaked 8-12 hrs
- 1 carob crust (p 191) or plain pie crust (p 194)
- 8 apples
- 120 g/4 oz fresh dates, pitted
- 1 tbsp cinnamon
- 1 lemon, juiced
- 1 tbsp psyllium

Soak the sesame seeds in advance. Prepare your crust and line the sides and base of a 20 cm/8 in flan tin. Chop and core the apples; put the pieces in the blender and blend to a purée. Add the sesame seeds, dates, cinnamon, and lemon juice, and blend again. When you're confident that everything is mixed up and there are no seedy bits left, add the psyllium. Blend for another minute. Pour into your crust, smooth out the top, and leave in the fridge to set for a couple of hours.

■ ■ ■ ■ The apple season in the UK is quite long, roughly from September to April. Enjoy them throughout the winter, but in the summer, minimize your intake of the imported varieties from New Zealand and America and enjoy the strawberries and raspberries instead.

- 1 hr, soaking 8-12 hrs, setting 2 hrs
- Food processor, blender
- **Serves twelve**

■ Poppy Seed Tart

Poppy seeds are a wonderful addition to salads and sweet dishes, just a sprinkle adds crunchy texture and a light nutty flavour to dishes.

- 120 g/4 oz sunflower seeds, soaked 1-2 hrs
- 120 g/4 oz dates
- 1 tsp cinnamon
- 120 g/4 oz apricots, soaked 4 hrs
- 60 g/2 oz dates
- 1 tsp vanilla extract
- 150 g/5 oz almonds, soaked 8-12 hrs
- 4 bananas
- 125 ml/4 fl oz agave syrup
- 125 ml/4 fl oz olive oil
- 125 ml/4 fl oz water
- 2 tbsp psyllium
- 200 g/7 oz poppy seeds

To make the crust, put the sunflower seeds in the food processor and process until they are as ground down as you can get them. Then add the dates and cinnamon, and process again until you have a dough. Press the mixture into a large flan dish, to form a crust on the base and sides. Clean out the food processor, and put the apricots, second lot of dates, and vanilla in. Process until the apricots and dates are amalgamated, and press into your sunflower crust, to make a layer on the bottom. Next in the blender, put the almonds, bananas (peeled and broken into pieces), agave, olive oil, and water. Blend to a thick cream, then add the psyllium and blend for a further minute. By hand, stir in the poppy seeds, making sure you mix them evenly right through the mixture. The mixture should be quite solid. Spread it on the top of the apricot layer, quickly before it firms up completely. Pop it in the fridge to set for a couple of hours.

- 45 mins, setting 2 hrs
- Food processor, blender
- **Serves twelve**

■ Ethan's Cake

Ethan invented this recipe for his fourth birthday. He was born in January, so there's not much fruit around, and this is what he came up with. It sounds pretty plain, but the flavours do amazing things together, and it actually turned out to be one of our favourite cakes.

- 150 g/5 oz almonds, ground
- 120 g/4 oz fresh dates, pitted
- 1 tbsp carob powder
- 2 large or 3 small apples
- 2 large or 3 small pears
- 2 lemons
- 4 bananas
- 1 tbsp psyllium husk powder
- 120 g/4 oz Lexia raisins

To prepare the crust, grind the almonds in a coffee grinder or high power blender. Mash the dates in the food processor. Once they've formed a sticky mass, add the carob and the almonds and process again until it's all mixed together in a gorgeous brown goo. Press it into the cake tin, the base and up the sides, and try not to lick your fingers until you've finished.

Prepare the apples and pears by removing the cores and chopping them so they'll fit in the chute of your food processor. Using the fine slicing blade, slice the fruit. Put them in a mixing bowl. Juice the lemons, and add to the blender with the bananas. Blend until there are no lumps left. Add the psyllium, and blend for another minute. Pour it into the bowl with the fruit. Add the Lexias, and stir it up, so the fruit is well mixed. Spoon it into your crust, flatten the top and leave to set in the fridge for a couple of hours.

■ ■ ■ ■ Pears top the list of foods that people are least likely to be allergic to, so they make a great first food for babies.

- 1 hr, dehydrating 12-18 hrs
- Blender, dehydrator
- **Serves twelve**

The Best Birthday Cake

This makes a dense sponge cake, resembling a Victoria sandwich.

Cake:
- 360 g/12 oz wheat grain, sprouted
- 90 g/3 oz carob powder
- 250 ml/8 fl oz olive oil
- 125 ml/4 fl oz agave nectar
- 125 ml/4 fl oz water

Filling:
- 4 bananas
- 2 lemons
- 1 tbsp psyllium

Icing:
- 200 g/7 oz tahini
- 2 bananas
- 60 g/2 oz carob powder

Decoration:
- 1 tbsp Lexia raisins
- 1 tbsp coconut chips
- 1 tbsp goji berries

Sprout the wheat three days in advance. To make the cake, put all the first set of ingredients into the blender and whiz to a batter. Spread a third of the mixture on a dehydrator sheet in a large circle. Repeat with the rest of the batter, so you have three large circles which more or less fill each sheet. Dehydrate for 12–18 hrs.

Once cooled, slide one round onto a plate or cake tray, whatever you want to serve it on because you will not be able to move it again. Blend the bananas with the juice of the lemons and, once puréed, add the psyllium. Working quickly before the psyllium sets, spoon half of the lemon mix onto the round. Put the second round on top, then repeat, so you have three layers – cake, lemon filling, cake, lemon filling, cake.

Then it's back to the blender to mix the tahini, carob, and bananas. This needs to be quite thick so it will stick to the sides of the cake. Using a knife, smooth it over the top and around the edge, so it looks like a proper iced cake.

Decorate with Lexia raisins, coconut chips and goji berries. Add the required number of candles and there you have it – a birthday cake fit for your little prince or princess!

■ ■ ■ ■ Like currants and sultanas, Lexias are just a different variety of dried grape. Fat and juicy, I have never seen organic ones for sale, but they make a lovely change from the standard variety in puddings, sweets and chocolate.

- 45 mins
- Blender, food processor
- **Serves sixteen**

■ Carob Torte

This recipe is an adapted version of one in Juliano's book, *Raw: The Uncook Book*. Fabulous as his is, it is incredibly rich – this is toned down but still very decadent.

- 180 g/6 oz walnuts, ground
- 120 g/4 oz raisins
- 1 tbsp cinnamon
- 250 g/8 oz fresh coconut pieces
- 420 g/14 oz fresh dates, pitted
- 125 ml/4 fl oz agave nectar
- 250 g/8 oz cashews, ground
- 200 g/7 oz carob powder
- 2 lemons
- 4 bananas
- 250 g/8 oz seasonal fruit

This cake has four layers: crust, filling, icing and topping. To begin by making the crust, take the walnuts, raisins, and cinnamon. Mash the raisins in the food processor, until they form a solid mass. Add the nuts and cinnamon, and process until the nuts and raisins are completely mixed together. Press into a flan dish, just lining the base, not the sides.

Clean the food processor and put the coconut pieces in. Process until it's evenly broken down into small pieces, the size of raisins or rice grains. Remove from the food processor, and put in a large mixing bowl. Process the dates until they form a ball. With the machine running, gradually add the agave to the dates. Once it's all mixed together, add to the mixing bowl with your coconut chips, ground cashews, and carob powder. With a wooden spoon, mix everything together until the mixture is stiff. Spoon it into your dish, on top of the crust.

Juice the lemons, and pour the juice in the blender with the bananas, peeled and broken into pieces. Blend until there are no lumps of banana left. Pour this over your torte. Finally, arrange your fruit on top: mixed berries are great in the summer, or clementine segments in the winter. You can serve it straight away, or keep it in the fridge for up to a week.

■ ■ ■ ■ Carob pods are so plentiful in southern Spain, farmers do not know what to do with them and use them as animal feed.

- 20 mins, soaking 8 -12 hrs, dehydrating 24 hrs
- Blender, dehydrator
- **Serves eight**

■ Malt Loaf

At The Tree of Life Rejuvenation Center in the USA, they make breads and loaves based on flax seeds. When I tried one of their recipes, I found it very reminiscent of malt loaf. This is my adaptation – it's delightfully squidgy and substantial without being sickly.

- 60 g/2 oz figs, soaked 4-8 hrs
- 60 g/2 oz apricots, soaked 4-8 hrs
- 180 g/6 oz walnuts, soaked 8-12 hrs
- 120 g/4 oz almonds, soaked 8-12 hrs
- 1 tbsp cinnamon
- 1 tbsp mixed spice
- 4 tbsp yacon syrup or molasses
- 300 g/10 oz flax seed, ground

Soak your figs, apricots, walnuts and almonds in advance. When they're ready, drain them off. You should discard the soak water from the nuts, but you can drink the water from the dried fruit, it's delicious. Put everything bar the flax seeds in the blender. The nuts and dried fruits should have absorbed enough water to make the mixture runny enough to blend. Spoon it out into a mixing bowl, and stir in the flax seeds with a spoon. They will stiffen the mixture considerably. Transfer it to a drying tray, and mould it into a loaf shape, about 5 cm/2 in high (no taller, or it won't dry through properly). Dry for 12 hrs, then turn it over so the bottom side gets done too, and dry for a further 12 hrs. Serve with raw nut butter for a teatime snack.

■ ■ ■ ■ The Tree of Life Center was founded in 1993 by Dr Gabriel Cousens, and has come to be one of the foremost focal points for raw food teaching in the world. It is set in 182 acres of land and is home to people from over 100 nations.

- 45 mins, sprouting, 24 hrs dehydrating
- Juicer, blender, dehydrator
- **Serves eight**

■ Chocolate Cake

Out of all the cakes, this is by far my favourite, reminiscent of those Victoria sponges we grew up on. I originally wrote the recipe using carob, but since then the wondrous cacao bean has appeared.

- 180 g/6 oz wheat, sprouted
- 150 g/5 oz fresh dates, pitted
- 120 g/4 oz cacao nibs
- 125 ml/4 fl oz olive oil
- 1 banana
- 1 avocado
- 2 tbsp agave nectar
- 2 tbsp raw chocolate powder

You really need a juicer for this, nothing else will mash up the wheat sprouts. Put them through with the blank plate on, followed by the dates and the cacao nibs if you're using them. In a large mixing bowl, knead the sprouts, dates, carob and grain coffee/cacao, and olive oil all together. Your hands are really the best tool here. When it's done, divide the mixture into two halves. On drying trays, shape into rounds about 5 cm/2 in deep and 20 cm/8 in in diameter. Dehydrate for 12 hrs. Take two clean drying trays, and flip the cakes over to make sure they dry on the other side. Dehydrate for a further twelve hours.

When they're done, you're ready to make the filling. Peel the banana, break it into pieces, and put it in the blender. Scoop out the avocado flesh, and add that to the blender along with the agave and carob. Blend up to a cream – add a little water if you're having difficulty. Slide one of your cakes onto a serving plate. Spoon the cream on top, nice and thick. Slide the second cake on top, and it's ready to eat.

- 45 mins
- Food processor, blender
- **Serves twelve**

■ Reuben's Cake

Not to be outdone, here's the recipe Reuben came up with for his birthday that same year. He has a summer birthday, so we made the most of the wonderful seasonal berries. As this cake's quite solid, you aren't restricted to using a cake tin. You can make it on a tray or large plate, and mould it into whatever shape you wish – a heart or a star – Reuben had a number seven because it was his seventh birthday.

- 120 g/4 oz sunflower seeds, ground
- 120 g/4 oz hemp seeds, ground
- 120 g/4 oz raisins
- 60 g/2 oz carob powder
- 1 large mango
- 2 nectarines
- 1 lemon, juiced
- 1 tbsp psyllium husk powder
- 120 g/4 oz cashews, ground
- 120 g/4 oz fresh dates, pitted
- 500 g/1 lb strawberries
- 250 g/8 oz raspberries
- 250 g/8 oz blueberries

This cake has four layers. To make the base, grind the sunflower and hemp seeds in a coffee grinder or high power blender. Mash the raisins in the food processor. Then add the sunflower seeds and hemp seeds and process until they are evenly mixed. Next add the carob powder and process again. If it doesn't stick together, you may want to add a few drops of water. Press it down flat onto your serving tray.

Next is the fruit layer. Remove the mango flesh from the stone, and peel off the skins. Put the flesh in the blender, along with the nectarines, pitted and chopped, and lemon juice. The resulting mixture will be quite liquid. Add the psyllium and blend again. Leave it to one side for a few minutes so it starts to thicken. Once it's gone to jelly, spoon it onto the seed base.

For the third layer, mash the dates in the food processor. Once they're a solid mass, add the cashews and combine. Spread this layer on top of your now set jelly layer. Finally, press the berries into the cake, completely covering the top and sides. The result is a beautiful berry feast – too good for anyone to turn down.

■ ■ ■ ■ There are hundreds of varieties of mango grown worldwide – India is the main producer. Tommy Atkins is the most common, accounting for 80% of those sold in the UK, while the Alfonso is the most prized for its fragrant delicate flavour.

- 45 mins, 2 hrs setting
- Food processor, blender
- **Serves twelve**

■ Coconut Torte

This was a real favourite in our house for a while. Rich and yet somehow light at the same time. Coconut is wonderfully health giving, we eat a lot of it. Full of lauric acid, a highly beneficial fatty acid, it balances the metabolism and so it's a fat that you can eat a lot of without putting on weight.

- 180 g/6 oz walnuts, ground
- 2 fresh coconuts (p 77)
- 120 g/4 oz raisins
- 1 tbsp cinnamon
- 90 g/3 oz carob powder
- 250 g/8 oz fresh dates, pitted
- 2 tsp tamari
- 2 tbsp grain coffee
- 125 ml/4 fl oz olive oil
- 125 ml/4 fl oz agave nectar
- 250 ml/8 fl oz water
- 250 g/8 oz raspberries

Grind the walnuts in a coffee grinder or high power blender. Extract the coconut meat from the shells. To prepare the base, take the walnuts, raisins, cinnamon, and 120 g/4 oz of coconut meat. Mash the raisins in the food processor until you have a solid mass. Then add the coconut and grind some more. Once all the coconut's worked in, add the ground walnuts and cinnamon, and process until everything is evenly combined. Press the mixture into your flan dish, making just a flat layer on the bottom.

Next put the remaining coconut meat, carob, dates, tamari, grain coffee, olive oil, agave and water in the blender. You should have enough liquid that it doesn't have a problem turning over. If you have a standard high street blender, you might have a bit of a problem; maybe mash the dates and coconut in the food processor first. You don't want to add any more water or it will be too runny. The result should be a very thick, slightly granular cream. Spoon it into your flan dish, levelling out the top, and decorating with the fresh raspberries. Leave to set for an hour or two before serving.

■ ■ ■ ■ In southern Thailand, a type of monkey called the pig-tailed macaque is trained to harvest the coconuts from the palms, and competitions are held to find the fastest harvester.

- 40 mins, sprouting, soaking 8-12 hrs, dehydrating 18 hrs
- Blender, dehydrator, ice cream maker
- **Serves twelve to sixteen**

■ Ice Cream Layer Cake

Call me crazy and slightly obsessive, but it's long been a fantasy of mine to make a raw arctic roll; this is pretty similar, and very gorgeous. Makes a perfect summer birthday cake.

Cake layer:
- 300 g/10 oz buckwheat, sprouted (see p 42)
- 90 g/3 oz carob powder or 120 g/4 oz ground cacao nibs
- 2 tbsp agave nectar
- 250 ml/8 fl oz water

Ice cream layer:
- 200 g/7 oz cashews, soaked 8-12 hrs
- 8 fresh dates, pitted
- 1 tbsp vanilla extract
- 250 ml/8 fl oz water

Icing:
- 2 tbsp almond butter
- 2 tbsp agave nectar
- 1 tbsp carob powder

Decoration:
- 2 tbsp goji berries
- 90 g/3 oz fresh berries if they're in season

Sprout the buckwheat two or three days in advance. Soak the cashews overnight. To make the cake, put all the first set of ingredients in the blender and blend to a cream. Spoon it out onto three drying trays, and shape into large circles, which should take up most of the tray. The important thing is that they are more or less the same size as you are going to stack them one on the other. Dry the rounds for 12 hrs, then flip over (hold a second, clean tray on top and then turn them upside down, and remove the first tray). Dry for another 6 hrs.

To make the ice cream, blend all the second set of ingredients together to a cream, and pour into your ice cream maker. Mine takes about 20 mins of churning to turn nut cream into ice cream. It needs to be quite solid, but still spreadable.

Slide a cake layer onto a large plate, and spoon half the ice cream over the top to make a nice thick layer, spreading it right the way to the edge. Slide the second cake layer on top, and cover that with the remaining ice cream. Slide the third cake layer on top.

Make the icing by mixing the almond butter, agave and carob in a bowl with a spoon. If it's not runny enough to spread, add water. Using a knife or a spoon, spread it thinly over the top of the cake. Decorate with goji berries, or whatever fruit is in season – strawberries are a winner. Eat immediately. Store leftovers in the freezer – to eat, remove 20 mins before you're ready to allow it to defrost and soften a little so you can cut yourself a slice.

■ ■ ■ ■ The Americans eat the most ice cream of any nation in the world – on average 23 litres a year. In the UK, we measure up with a measly 6 litres.

■ Cookies

In this chapter we celebrate sweet biscuits you can eat as many of as you like without worrying about putting on weight, or clogging up your arteries, or getting a sugar overdose. Eating raw cookies is such a joy – not only are you feeding your body nutrient dense goodies it loves, you are liberating your mind too! I was brought up almost to be scared of biscuits - they were always around, part of the daily diet, but to be monitored and carefully controlled, for fear of going over my calorie count for the day, or getting spots, or spoiling my appetite for dinner. To be able to eat as many sweet snacks as your heart desires without a trace of guilt is a wonderful experience everyone deserves to have. Make a batch, share them with your friends, and spread the joy.

- 5 mins, pre-soaking 8-12 hrs, dehydrating 24 hrs
- Blender, dehydrator
- **Makes about 25 biscuits**

Strawberry Shortcake

Lovely melt in the mouth summer biscuits, for when the strawberries are in season. You can substitute any berry for the strawberries: blueberries and raspberries are gorgeous.

- 300 g/10 oz Brazil nuts, pre-soaked 8-12 hrs
- 200 g/7 oz strawberries
- 60 g/2 oz dates, pitted
- 4 tbsp olive oil
- 125-250 ml/4-8 fl oz water
- 2 tsp cinnamon

Soak your Brazils in advance. Dice the strawberries into tiny pieces, about the size of a raisin. Mix everything else in the blender and purée so there are no bits of nut left. Use as little water as possible, or your biscuits will be too soggy. Stir in the berries by hand. Spread the mixture onto a dehydrating tray. Dry for 12 hrs, and then score into about 25 biscuits (five across by five down). Turn, and dry for another 12 hrs. Stored in an airtight tin in the fridge, they will keep for up to a week.

■ ■ ■ ■ If you have the time and inclination, these biscuits are even better if you dry the berries first. Dice them, spread on a tray, and dry for 6-12 hrs. Then add the dried berries into the mix, so you end up with a chewier berry in the finished cookie.

- 10 mins, 8-12 hrs pre-soaking and 18 hrs dehydrating
- Blender, dehydrator
- **Makes 24 buns**

Hot Cross Buns

Hot cross buns are one of those seasonal treats it's often hard to let go of. The aromatic spices, the chewy dried fruit, the doughy bun.... So I had to come up with a raw version.

- 300 g/10 oz oats, pre-soaked 8-12 hrs
- 4 tbsp agave nectar
- 4 tbsp olive oil
- 2 tbsp mixed spice
- 250 ml/8 fl oz water
- 200 g/7 oz mixed vine fruit

Cross:
- 2 tbsp yacon syrup or molasses
- 2 tbsp tahini
- Water to mix

Soak the oats overnight. You can use oat groats or rolled oats, whichever you prefer. Put everything in the blender apart from the dried fruit, and blend to a thick batter. Stir in the vine fruit by hand. Using a teaspoon, put dollops of the mixture on the dehydrator tray, nice and fat, like little buns. They should ideally be about 2 cm/1 in high, and 6 cm/3 in diameter. Dry for 18 hrs. When they're done, mix up the tahini and molasses with a spoon or two of water so it is not too stiff to spread, and not so runny that it won't stick. Using a teaspoon, you should be able to drizzle a cross on top of the buns.

■ ■ ■ ■ Yacon syrup is available from the online raw food stores. It is a sugar-free sweetener made from a Peruvian root vegetable, which tastes similar to barley malt syrup but has no impact on the blood sugar.

■ 15 mins and pre-soaking 8-12 hrs and dehydrating 16 hrs
■ Blender, dehydrator
■ **Makes about 40 biscuits**

■ Lovely Biscuits

The great thing about these is they are sweet without containing too much sugary stuff. Stevia is a herb which is 30–100 times sweeter than sugar. So a few drops of it will do in your cakes and biscuits instead of any other sweetener. If you taste it straight from the bottle or packet, it's not very nice, like strong molasses, but in a recipe, it is one of the healthiest and least sickly sweeteners you can find. Unfortunately, you can't buy it in this country, so you'd have to ask a friend in North America to send some over for you.

■ 150 g/5 oz Brazils, soaked 8-12 hrs
■ 150 g/5 oz flax seeds, soaked 8-12 hrs
■ 20 drops stevia or 2 tsp stevia powder
■ 1 tsp cinnamon
■ 120 g/4 oz raisins

Soak the nuts and seeds overnight in 1 litre (32 fl oz) of water. Put them in the blender with the stevia and cinnamon, and blend until there are no seeds discernable in the mix. Stir in the raisins by hand. Spread onto dehydrator trays, and dry for 12 hrs. Slice, turn and dry for 2-4 hrs more.

■ ■ ■ ■ These were our favourites for a long while. I didn't know what to call them until Ethan asked for one of those 'lovely biscuits' one day and the name stuck.

- 10 mins, 12 hrs dehydrating
- Blender, food processor, dehydrator
- **Makes about 20 cookies**

■ Coconut Carob Cookies

- 250 g/8 oz dates, pitted
- 2 bananas, peeled and chopped
- 60 g/2 oz carob powder or raw chocolate powder
- 270 g/9 oz fresh coconut

Blend dates, banana and carob together to a purée. Chop the coconut into small pieces, and grate it in the food processor, so you have small chunks no bigger than a raisin. Stir into the carob mix by hand. Put spoonfuls of the mixture onto the dehydrator trays, flattening down so they are not too thick – ideally about 1 cm/^{1}/$_2$ in. Dry for 12 hrs.

- 5 mins, 8-12 hrs pre-soaking, 12 hrs dehydrating
- Blender, dehydrator
- **Makes twelve**

■ Apple Cashew Cookies

- 120 g/4 oz cashews, pre-soaked 8-12 hrs
- 500 g /1 lb apples
- 120 g/4 oz raisins

Pre-soak the cashews. If you forget, you can just grind them up and add them to the mix – it will still work fine. Chop the apples into pieces that are manageable for your blender. Blend the apples and cashews together, and once you've got a purée, with no bits of nut remaining, stir in the raisins by hand. Put spoonfuls on your dehydrator tray, about 1 cm/^{1}/$_2$ in high. Dry for 12 hrs, flip, and dry for another 6 hrs.

- 10 mins, 8-12 hrs pre-soaking, 18 hrs drying
- Blender, dehydrator
- **Makes sixteen**

Chocolate Brownies

These are based around the flapjack recipe from *Eat Smart Eat Raw*. There are a lot of recipes in that book that I still use on a daily basis, and the flapjacks are one of them. But this has to be the king! Using the wondrous cacao bean, these taste so good, as well as giving you such a hit of pure cacao magic.

- 300 g/10 oz oats, soaked 8-12 hrs
- 120 g/4 oz cacao, ground
- 120 g/4 oz fresh dates, pitted
  (or 4 tbsp agave syrup and 125 ml/4 fl oz water)
- 125 ml/4 fl oz olive oil
- 1 tbsp maca powder (optional, for an extra buzz)
- 2 tbsp carob powder
- 4 tbsp carob chips (not raw, optional)

Pre-soak the oats. You can use rolled oats or groats, whichever you prefer. Put all the ingredients apart from the carob chips in the blender, and process to a thick purée. Stir in the carob chips or raisins by hand. Spoon the mixture onto a dehydrating tray, about 1 cm/$1/2$ in thick. Form into a square shape. Dry for 12 hrs and then score into 16 squares (four by four). Turn, and dry for a further 6 hrs. Stored in an airtight container in the fridge, they will keep for a couple of weeks.

■ ■ ■ These make a great mid-morning snack, as the oats stabilize blood sugar levels for the day and the cacao gives you a boost to help you breeze through to lunch.

- 10 mins, 12 hrs dehydrating
- Blender, dehydrator
- **Makes twelve**

■ Carrot Cakes

The ground flax seeds give these a kind of yeasty taste that along with the spices and dried fruit makes them just like little buns.

- 150 g/5 oz flax seeds, ground
- 1 apple
- 4 carrots
- 1 tbsp mixed spice
- 2 tbsp raisins

Grind the flax seeds in a coffee grinder or high power blender. Chop and core the apple; top and tail the carrots. Chop them into blender-friendly sized pieces, pop them in, and purée them. Add the ground flax seeds and mixed spice and purée again. Stir in the raisins by hand. You should have a fairly firm mixture. Shape it into patties between the palms of your hands, getting them as thin as you can without them falling apart. You should have about a dozen little cakes. Spread on a drying tray and dry for six hours, turn over and dry for another six hours.

■ ■ ■ ■ Carrots were the first vegetable to be canned, in the early 19th century.

- 10 mins, 8-12 hrs soaking, 18 hrs dehydrating
- Blender, dehydrator
- **Makes 20**

Flapjacks

OK, I'm cheating; these were in *Eat Smart Eat Raw*. But they're so good; they're worth drawing your attention to again. And I have tinkered with the recipe slightly.

- 300 g/10 oz oats, soaked 8-12 hours
- 4 tbsp agave nectar
- 4 tbsp olive oil
- 4 tbsp water
- 120 g/4 oz raisins

Put everything except for the raisins in the blender. Blend to a porridge (you can eat it like this for breakfast if you want!). Stir in the raisins by hand. Spread onto a drying tray, about 2 cm/1 in thick. Dry for 12 hrs, then score into squares, four by five, or possibly five by five if you want to make little ones. Flip over, and dry for a further six hours. Store in an airtight container, and keep for up to two weeks.

Variations: Honestly, we make these every week and we never get bored of them. Try blending in:

- 2 tbsp carob powder
- 2 tbsp goji berries, soaked 1-2 hrs
- 2 tbsp bee pollen
- 2 tbsp maca powder
- 2 tbsp fresh dates instead of agave
- 1 tbsp cinnamon, or mixed spice
- 2 cm/1 in fresh root ginger
- 10 drops orange oil

■ ■ ■ ■ Oats are such a great snack because they're a slow-release carbohydrate, giving you sustained energy levels, rather than a quick hit and then a dip like a sugary snack will give you.

■ Sweets

Some little nibbles that should be enough to persuade even the most reluctant among you that raw food isn't boring and bland. Whip these out to impress guests, children, or on birthdays or at Christmas – in fact at every available opportunity. These are sweets that you can eat without worrying about ruining your appetite – they have more nutrition in them than a 'proper meal' like pasta and jarred sauce or a frozen dinner.

- 30 mins
- Food processor or gear juicer
- **Makes 25**

Special Sweeties

Pine nuts and macadamias together is a gorgeously decadent combination, rich and luxurious and positively naughty! If your budget won't stretch to both, you could substitute hulled sesame seeds for one or the other.

- 120 g/4 oz pine nuts
- 120 g/4 oz macadamia nuts
- 120 g/4 oz fresh dates, pitted
- 1 tbsp agave nectar
- 90 g/3 oz carob powder
- Pinch sea salt

There are two ways of making these. The best way is to feed them through a gear juicer with the blank plate on, nuts first then dates. Add a pinch of sea salt to the mixing bowl, and using a spoon or your hands mix everything together. If you don't have a gear juicer, you can grind the nuts first, and then put everything together in the food processor. You don't get as smooth a sweet, but it still works. Take the mixture and form into walnut-sized balls. Store in the fridge – they will keep for a few weeks.

■ ■ ■ ■ For Valentine's Day, or as a gift for a loved one, shape them into hearts, about 1 cm/^{1}/$_2$ in thick and 3 cm/1 in long, then pour some melted chocolate or carob over the top for icing.

- 20 mins
- Gear juicer, food processor
- **Makes 25-30 truffles**

■ Super Sweeties

These have got everything going on in there. Wonderful for parties to get everyone in a lively festive spirit. What's more, they're so packed with vitamins and minerals; you could virtually live on them.

- 250 g/8 oz cacao nibs
- 90 g/3 oz goji berries
- 2 tbsp maca powder
- 2 tbsp bee pollen granules
- 1 tbsp Klamath Lake blue-green algae powder
- 2 tbsp agave syrup
- 60 g/2 oz carob powder
- Pinch crystal or sea salt

If you have a gear juicer, put the cacao and gojis through with the blank plate on. If not grind the cacao in a grinder, and mash the gojis separately in the food processor. Then put everything together in the food processor, and keep it turning until the mixture balls up. If it doesn't start sticking, add a few drops of water to help it along. Once you've got a solid mass, break off small pieces and shape into walnut-sized balls. Stored in an airtight container in the fridge, they should keep for up to a month.

■ ■ ■ ■ Our favourite type of blue-green algae is called Crystal Manna. It comes as flakes and looks just like green glitter – it has to be seen to be believed. We sprinkle it on our dinner or add it to our chocolate.

- 30 mins
- Food processor
- **Makes 20 pieces** (or one if you're my ex-husband)

■ Raw Chocolate

The cacao bean is what all chocolate is made from. The raw bean is
a relative newcomer to the raw food scene, first being imported
commercially into this country in 2004. It's so good, I wouldn't be
surprised if they tried to make it illegal. I can't get enough of it -
it makes me feel happier, full of energy, more productive, less hungry.
For a decadent, delectable sweet try this truffle recipe.

- 120 g/4 oz cacao beans or nibs
- 120 g/4 oz sesame seeds
- 1 vanilla pod
- 120 g/4 oz fresh dates, pitted

Grind up the cacao, sesame seeds and vanilla in a food grinder or high
powered blender. Mash the dates up in the food processor. We only use
120 g/4 oz dates, which makes a very deep chocolatey truffle, a bit like
plain chocolate. If you have a sweet tooth, you may want to add more
dates or a tablespoon of agave nectar. Add the vanilla, sesame seed
and cacao mixture to the food processor and turn until it balls up.
Break into walnut sized pieces and form into small balls. If they're for a
gift or a party, coat them in desiccated coconut for a professional
finish. Alternatively, you can just leave it in one big lump and eat huge
chunks like my ex-husband does. Whichever way, it needs to be stored
in the fridge.

■ ■ ■ ■ Raw Living was the first company to retail raw chocolate bars
in the UK. Now there are dozens on the market. If your local
health food store doesn't stock them, ask them to get some
in. Once people get into the raw chocolate habit, invariably
they don't want to go back to the cooked stuff.

- 5 mins, 12 hrs drying
- Blender, dehydrator
- **Makes four**

Green Leathers

How many people do you know that will gladly eat kale? In my quest to get more greens in my boys, I came up with these, containing a decent serving of kale, but the end result just tastes like a sweet treat.

- 4 apples
- 500 g/1 lb kale

Chop the apples, remove the cores. Put the apple pieces in the blender, and blend to a purée. Then prepare the kale: discard any large stems, chop into little bits, and add to the apple purée. Purée until you have no bits left, and the mix is a gorgeous deep green. Spread onto a dehydrator tray and dry for 12 hrs, until it will peel smoothly off the tray. Roll up, and then slice them into two across the middle. Store in an airtight container in a cool place. Will keep for up to a month.

Salad Bar

Similar to Green Leather but this is a salad in a snack bar.

- 1 apple
- 2 sticks celery
- 4 leaves lettuce
- 1 tomato
- 1/2 cucumber

Prepare the lot for the blender by chopping into manageable chunks. Discard the apple core. If you're using leafy celery, remove the leaves: they are health-giving, but bitter, and will overpower the flavour of the bar. Toss everything in the blender, and whiz it up to a liquid.

Have a taste: if it's not sweet enough for you, add an extra apple.
Spread onto two drying trays, and dry for 12 hrs. When they're pliable, not at all soggy (underdone) or crisp (overdone), they're ready.
Take them out, roll them up and slice them into two across the middle.
Store in an airtight container in the fridge. Will keep for up to a month.

- 5 mins, soaking 4-8 hrs
- Blender
- **Makes two jars**

■ Jam

For spreading on crackers or Essene bread, this tastes just like those sugar-free fruit jams you can buy, and is so quick and easy to make.

- 60 g/2 oz prunes, soaked 4-8 hrs
- 3 apples
- 1 lemon, juiced

Soak the prunes in advance. Core and chop the apples, put the pieces in the blender. Blend until you have a purée. Add the prunes and lemon juice, and purée again. Stored in jars in the fridge, will keep for about 5 days.

■ ■ ■ ■ **Variation:** replace the prunes with unsulphured dried apricots for apricot jam.

- 10 mins
- **Makes 16 balls**

■ Maca Balls

Maca is a fantastic superfood (see p 25) full of protein and minerals and very energising. Its flavour goes very well with carob. Have one (or two) of these mid-morning or late afternoon when you're starting to flag, to perk you up.

- 2 heaped tbsp maca powder
- 60 g/2 oz carob powder
- 250 g/8 oz tahini
- 2 tbsp agave

Put the whole lot in a mixing bowl, and combine with a spoon. Roll into walnut-sized balls – makes about 16. Stored in an airtight container in the fridge, they should keep for weeks.

■ ■ ■ ■ The maca plant grows at higher altitudes than any other plant in the world. It can also withstand extremes of temperature – intense heat and biting cold. So it provides us with that energy of endurance, of being able to battle through life no matter how high the mountain or how fierce the storm.

■ Guest recipes

Raw is getting more and more popular by the day, which is
fantastic. But the number of people who have been doing it
a long time is actually quite small. Ten years ago it was very
hard to sustain the diet when there was so little information
and support around, and many people who believed that this
way of eating is beneficial found they couldn't integrate it
into their existing lifestyles, or didn't have the knowledge
to make it work for them. That's why those people who have
stuck at it over the years really deserve recognition and
support. They are pioneers, making mistakes and learning
the hard way, so they can share their lessons with you.
Here is a selection of recipes by some of my very favourite
people on the planet. Tuck in.

Holly Paige

■ Golden Cherry Cream Pie

Holly is a big fan of raw dairy produce for her growing children. Most raw fooders are vegan, but Holly and others find raw dairy such as unpasteurised goats' cheese and yoghurt an essential part of the road to optimum health.

'Pastry'

- ■ 90 g/3 oz almonds, soaked
- ■ 90 g/3 oz hazelnuts/ filberts, soaked and dehydrated if possible
- ■ 5 dates, fresh if possible
- ■ 5 prunes
- ■ 1 banana
- ■ 30 g/1 oz pitted dried cherries or goji berries if not available
- ■ Handful cacao nibs

Topping

- ■ 200 ml/7 fl oz hemp milk made with 90 g/3 oz hemp seeds and juice of 2 oranges and extra water as necessary
- ■ A few pieces orange peel/zest
- ■ 2 dried figs
- ■ 1/2 banana
- ■ 60 g/2 oz macadamia nuts
- ■ 30 g/1 oz goji berries
- ■ Handful fresh cherries
- ■ Sprinkling chocolate powder

Process all the pastry ingredients except the cacao nibs together until smooth, mix in the nibs and form the pastry base on a plate. Blend the topping ingredients together until smooth and fill the pie. It will set in a few minutes. Sprinkle the raw chocolate powder on the top and decorate with halved cherries.

Steve Charter

◼ A Different Kind of Recipe for Salad Success

Steve is a long term raw foodist who has been actively promoting the benefits of the diet for well over a decade. He comes from a permaculture background, and works hard to get raw foods recognized as an integral part of sustainable living.

Take the seeds of a wide range of perennial and self-seeding salad plants – these might be rocket, lettuces, endive, different kales, tomatoes, perennial spinach, chard, oriental salad greens such as Mitsuna or mustard greens, chicory, celery, lovage, etc., and add a few seeds of edible flowers such as nasturtiums, mallow and calendula. Sprinkle these lightly in appropriate parts of the garden, in large pots or in window boxes. Add water. Add more water according to climatic needs on the days following the day of sowing and then as needed during the growth of the plants. Leave in the sun for 2 to 4 months, and then harvest and eat with some of the other fabulous recipes detailed in this book...

◼ ◼ ◼ ◼ Permaculture means permanent agriculture, and is a methodology of sustainable living which seeks to work in harmony with nature, and follow the patterns of ecology.

Jess Michael

■ Superfood 'Cookie Dough' Balls

Jess suffered from ME when she was younger, and used the raw food diet to help rid herself of this debilitating condition. Now she has her own business, puts on popular workshops, and even runs marathons!

I usually double or treble the batches of these great Cookie Dough Balls, as they just never seem to last for too long. If you put them in the fridge for a few hours afterwards, they go solid which makes for the best ever travel snack.

- 390 g/13 oz of your favourite nuts – cashew and almond work well together (soaked for at least $1/2$ hr)
- 4 large dessertspoons of coconut butter
- 120 g/4 oz raisins
- 60 g/2 oz fresh, juicy dates
- 3 tsp cinnamon
- Seeds from 1 vanilla pod
- $1/2$ tsp Atlantic / Himalayan Rock Salt (optional)
- 60 g/2 oz goji berries (optional, yet highly recommended)
- 4 tbsp raw chocolate powder/ground down raw cacao nibs
- 3 tbsp agave nectar (optional, as the mixture might be sweet enough for you already)

If your coconut butter is solid, melt it down into liquid over a low heat. Add all the ingredients to your food processor and mix until a dough-like texture occurs. Taste your creation, to check for sweetness and texture. You might want to add the agave, if it's not sweet enough. Or some more coconut butter if you want it to be more blended. Time to get messy! Get a good spoonful of 'cookie dough' at a time and roll it into a ball in the palms of your hands. Refrigerate or eat straight away... you choose.

Rob Hull

■ Mushroom and Seaweed Sauce

Rob is a good friend based in London who works full time promoting raw foods through the Funky Raw website and magazine.

- 30 g/1 oz sea spaghetti seaweed, soaked for about 20 mins
- 90 g/3 oz mushrooms
- 1 medium avocado

Chop the mushrooms and avocado and place in a blender with the sea spaghetti and the soak water and blend. This makes quite a rich sauce to serve with salad.

■ ■ ■ ■ Funky Raw was founded in 2004 by Tish Clifford, a long-term raw fooder and mother of two children, in order to provide a voice for the raw food movement in the UK, particularly those seeking to use raw foods as a vehicle for personal development and global change.

Mike Nash

■ Aggressive Health Anti-inflammatory Cocktail

Mike is one of the most dynamic raw men in the UK. His book *Aggressive Health* is ground-breaking and inspiring, explaining the powerful benefits of a raw diet combined with physical training and NLP mind techniques.

- ■ 1 head of celery
- ■ 1 cucumber
- ■ 400 g/13 oz kale
- ■ 1 cm/^{1}/$_2$ in ginger
- ■ 1 lemon, juiced
- ■ 1 tbsp Greens for Life (Barleygrass powder blend)
- ■ Two E3live ice cubes from ice cube bags (Klamath Lake blue-green algae)

Put the whole lot in a blender jug and blend to a thick green smoothie. I also chase with a teaspoon of MSM that I put on the centre of my tongue so it avoids the bitter taste buds, have 3 vitalzym capsules (a systemic enzyme supplement), and then attack the day.

■ ■ ■ ■ Ginger is a powerful anti-inflammatory food, the phycocyanin in E3live has powerful anti-inflammatory properties, MSM is a powerful anti-inflammatory agent, and Vitalzym is probably the best anti-inflammatory enzyme on the market. With inflammation at the heart of all of the major disease of civilization, you can see why this cocktail is 'Aggressive' in its health promoting benefits. This is something Mike has almost every day. He says, "If you ain't feelin' good after ^{1}/$_2$ litre of this magic potion, you're in trouble!"

Joel 'Cosmic CacaoBoy', Gazdar

■ Manhattan Sub-Cumber Sandwich

Joel makes the best food I have ever eaten. Ever.

Cucumber skins are high in silica. Silica (sand) is known as the beauty mineral, and is beneficial for elasticity of tissues and whole brain functioning.

- ■ 1 cucumber (wider girth preferable)
- ■ 60 g/2 oz freshly ground pumpkin seeds and/or hemp seeds
- ■ 1 tsp (virgin preferably stone crushed) olive oil or raw tahini
- ■ 1 tsp unpastuerised apple cider vinegar or lemon juice
- ■ 1 clove fresh garlic
- ■ 1 sprig fresh dill weed/coriander/basil
- ■ Sprinkle of caraway seed
- ■ 1 tsp raw (preferably wildflower/unfiltered) honey or dried (unsulphured) apricots
- ■ 1 tsp unrefined sea salt

Remove the tip from a cucumber (ridged or plain), preferably not too cold. Hollow out with appropriate diameter copper pipe, chopstick, or type of spoon used to scoop marrow out of bone, (by leaving one end sealed you lessen the chances of squirting the filling everywhere). Save the juicy seedy core for salad or a dressing.

To make the filling, take all the other ingredients and either mix in a bowl, grind in a blender, or mash in a mortar and pestle.

Stuff the length of the cuke till full, allow up to an hour for marinade to diffuse inside and enjoy.

■ ■ ■ ■ Cucumber is thought to derive from 'cowcumber', because at one time they were thought to be fit only for feeding to cows!

Gina Panayi

■ **Makes approximately 20 cakes**

■ Melomacarouna: 'Honey' Cakes

Gina is unique in approaching raw foods from a Greek culinary perspective. She takes traditional Greek dishes and makes raw adaptations. She can often be found at vegan fayres and markets where her stall always has a long queue.

- ■ 4 medjool dates
- ■ 250 ml/8 fl oz agave syrup
- ■ 250 ml/8 fl oz fresh orange juice
- ■ 2 tbsp orange zest
- ■ 450 g/15 oz ground almonds soaked overnight
- ■ 120 g/4 oz golden flax seeds, ground
- ■ 2 tsp cinnamon
- ■ 1 tsp Celtic sea salt
- ■ Crushed walnuts for decorating

Put the dates through the juicer and then place in the blender with the agave syrup, orange juice and zest. Blend together until all the ingredients are well mixed. Drain and rinse the almonds and feed through the juicer with the blank blade. Place in the food processor with the ground flax seed, cinnamon and salt and very briefly pulsate. Pour some of the liquid from the blender into the food processor and process while adding more liquid a little at a time until it all starts to bind and the mixture is evenly mixed together. Take small pieces of the mixture with your hands and form into oval biscuit shapes. Place the biscuits onto a dehydrator tray. Crush or lightly grind the walnuts and sprinkle on top of the biscuits and place in the dehydrator on 145°F for about 3 hours and then at 115°F for another 2 hrs. These cakes should be slightly crispy on the outside but soft and moist on the inside.

■ ■ ■ ■ Medjool dates are probably the most popular among raw fooders, plump and tender, one is a whole meal in itself. There are many other varieties available, especially in Middle Eastern grocers. Look for the yellow ones on the vine – they are usually hard, but take them home and let them ripen and they taste divine.

Shazzie

■ Toby Roamed

Shazzie is one of the most beautiful beings I have ever encountered, everything she does comes from the heart and she is doing amazing work in increasing the amount of love and joy in people's lives.
We don't fight over the crown to be the UK's most popular raw food writer and promoter, we like to get together and have a giggle over the whole thing instead.

- ■ 120 g/4 oz cacao nibs
- ■ 120 g/4 oz cashew nuts
- ■ 200 g/7 oz cacao butter
- ■ 60 g/2 oz raw carob powder
- ■ 4 tbsp raw agave nectar
- ■ 1 tsp of Blue Manna powder
- ■ 1 tsp of maca
- ■ 2 dessertspoons of coconut oil

Grind the cacao nibs into a fine powder. Grind the cashew nuts into a fine powder. Grate the white cacao butter and add to a bowl. Pour some warm water into another bowl and sit the bowl with the butter in into this bowl. Don't get water into your cacao butter. Wait until the butter has melted, and then add the other ingredients. Stir very well and then pour it into any pretty moulds.

■ ■ ■ ■ Oooh, this is so much like that triangular chocolate that we all love. Er, except this one's got masses of brain food in it.

Angela Stokes

■ Seductively Squished Salad

Angela's amazing weight loss story is an inspiration to thousands. Born and bred in the south of England, these days she is to be found travelling the globe, sharing her adventures with like-minded souls and recording the events on her popular website.

This is my current favourite salad, which I tend to prepare around the middle of the day to tank me up on raw nutrition for the rest of the daytime. It is a very easy and appealing recipe to prepare...

- Head of 1 romaine lettuce sliced into thin strips/a few good handfuls of young salad greens
- Small bunch of cilantro (coriander) chopped very finely
- $1/2$ cucumber, grated
- 2 carrots, grated
- $1/2$ red bell pepper, sliced into small chunks
- handful of dulse, shredded small
- juice of a lemon or lime
- 1 tsp kelp powder/pinch of Himalayan sea salt to taste
- flesh of 1 avocado, in rough pieces
- Any other 'garnishes' of choice – e.g. chopped chives, fresh sprouts, nuts etc

Combine all of the ingredients in a big bowl, then with your hand, squish the whole mixture together until it is all evenly distributed and the avocado has spread out through all the other ingredients, like a dressing. I love this method because it removes the need for any other salad dressing, like heavy oils and is so easy to prepare, with a minimum amount of fuss or equipment. I call this 'seductively squished salad' as you then get to lick the remaining ingredients from your hand after the squishing, if you so desire. Makes enough for one, or two, depending on how hungry (and friendly) you are.

Jill Swyers

Rich 'No' Chocolate Mousse

Jill is a Hippocrates health educator, and a much loved and respected member of the raw foods community. She divides her time between London, Portugal and Florida, holding raw workshops, retreats, and trainings.

- 150 g/5 oz walnuts (soaked in water overnight)
- 90 g/3 oz pine nuts (soaked in water overnight)
- 200 g/7 oz dates (soaked in water to just cover dates)
- 90 g/3 oz carob powder
- 1/2 soft avocado (if available)
- 1/2 lemon (freshly juiced)

Throw away water from nuts and rinse – drain. Process walnuts and pine nuts in food processor. Add dates. Add carob powder. Place in dish. Leave in refrigerator for 2 hrs or overnight. Decorate with raspberries, strawberries or edible flowers – ENJOY.

■ ■ ■ ■ At Hippocrates they are big advocates of indoor greens. These are seed trays planted with seeds which are allowed to sprout and germinate and are usually consumed when they are a week or two old. As well as the more commonly known barleygrass and wheatgrass, they also use buckwheat, sunflower and pea greens.

Ysanne Spevack

■ Lotus, Nori and Red Wine Salad

One of my oldest and dearest friends, Ysanne is a hugely talented food writer with a passion for organics. Currently residing in the US, she continues to share her wisdom with us back in the UK through her books and website.

This rich and decadent salad is a great winter warmer, due to the wine. It's a salad you can pull out of nowhere, as it's made entirely from ingredients you can keep in your store cupboard. It's so strongly flavoured; I recommend you eat it as a starter rather than a side dish. Invented in California, I was inspired by the mix of Japanese sushi culture found there alongside the local penchant for fine Napa Valley wines. A truly eccentrically English take on the Californian culinary scene. And yes, wine is raw!

- ■ 2 tbsp red wine
- ■ 2 tbsp olive oil
- ■ 1 tbsp tahini
- ■ 1 tbsp black sesame seeds
- ■ 120 g/4 oz dried lotus root, rehydrated
- ■ 2 big sheets of nori, torn into 1 cm/$1/2$ in squares

Shake the wine and oil together in a small container to form a dressing. Add the tahini, and mix in with a fork, squashing any lumps to blend it in. Then mix in the seeds, and pour the dressing over the lotus root. Leave to marinade for at least 20 mins before serving. Just before the salad is eaten, sprinkle on the nori.

■ ■ ■ ■ Lotus root is very nutritious and popular in both Chinese and Indian cuisine. The lotus flower is a symbol of divine beauty in Hindu and Buddhist cultures.

■ Further information about my guests who generously let me use their recipes

Steve Charter: author of *Eat More Raw*, sustainability consultant, proposer and co-founder of both EcoForest (a raw food eco-project in Spain from 2000-2005) and the Somerset Trust for Sustainable Development. See **www.eatmoreraw.com** and **www.sc2.org.uk**

Joel 'Cosmic CacaoBoy' Gazdar has been pioneering the evolution of raw foods towards 'SuperLifeFood' since 2000. He currently writes for the rawinspirations e-zine. Joel is the CEO of 'Sunshine Supernaturals' guiding people through purification transformations, using abundant resourcefulness. He has designed the cross pollination 'Project Alchemy' which is being built and launched in London in 2007 in partnership with all active raw food teachers, inventors, healers and artists. If you wish stay in touch by emailing **cosmiccacaoboy@yahoo.com**

Rob Hull has been eating raw food for 4 years. He does the Funky Raw shop, magazine and festival and runs raw food and wild food workshops. **www.funkyraw.com; www.rawrob.com; rob@funkyraw.com**

Jess Michael, The Raw Lifestyle Coach, is a motivating speaker, writer and chef. Jess is the founder of Total Raw Food, coaching those who wish to improve their diet. **www.totalrawfood.com**

Mike Nash is the author of *Aggressive Health and Peak Performance Health Educator*. **www.aggressivehealth.co.uk**

Holly Paige and her youngest two children, Bertie and Lizzy, have been almost all raw since summer 2001. Along the way she has been a raw food caterer and taught raw food preparation. Her passionate interest is in how food and plants affect the brain and consciousness and, with this in mind, is selling high vibrational foods and supplements through her on-line shop **www.oceanwavevibrations.com**. Contact **holly@rawcuisine.co.uk** or visit **www.rawcuisine.co.uk**

Gina Panayi's book is called *The Raw Greek*. You can contact her by emailing **gina@therawgreek.com** or find her website at **www.therawgreek.com**.

Shazzie is the managing director of Rawcreation Ltd, which publishes her books, retails over 700 true health products and imports the finest organic raw superfoods. Shazzie has written three books: *Detox Delights*, *Detox Your World*, and *Naked Chocolate*, co-authored with USA raw food guru David Wolfe. Shazzie and her daughter Evie live together in Cambridge, UK. She has been an ethical vegan since 1997, and a raw foodist since 2000. Being a raw foodist was an intrinsic part of her journey towards mental, spiritual and physical freedom. Due to her open, honest and personable writings, Shazzie attracts around 9,000 visitors to her website (**www.shazzie.com**) every day.

Ysanne Spevack loves food and this blue green planet. Her thirteen books all focus on organic food and organic living. They include: *Organic Cookbook*; *Fresh and Wild - A Real Food Adventure*; and *The Real Taste of Japan*; plus her industry report for Reuters about the international organic, functional and whole foods market. She is editor of the UK's leading organic foods website, **www.organicfood.co.uk** and was founding consultant editor of *Organic* magazine in the UK.

Angela Stokes lost more than 11 stone (150 lbs/70 kg) with a raw food lifestyle, reversing morbid obesity. She runs **www.rawreform.com**, where she shares her message of recovery through articles, e-books, lectures and natural weight loss retreats. She is passionate about helping others help themselves to reclaim better health and more vibrant lives. She can be contacted on **angela@rawreform.com**.

Jill Swyers is a fully trained Hippocrates health educator and nutritional and food consultant. She lectures on nutrition and holds residential detox retreats. You can contact her by visiting her website **www.jillswyers.com** or emailing **info@jillswyers.com**.

■ Resources

www.rawliving.co.uk, you can find information, advice, articles and recipes on the raw food lifestyle. Raw Living also runs regular workshops, lectures and parties featuring leading raw speakers from around the world. The Raw Living online shop sells a range of raw chocolate bars and superfoods.

You can find virtually all ingredients to build your raw food pantry on Shazzie's website **www.detoxyourworld.com**, telephone 08700 113 119. If they do not sell what you are after, then it probably means you can't buy it in the UK!

Kate and Shazzie are working together on setting up a raw foods community in the south of England. For more information visit: **www.theheartcentre.org.uk**.

■ Recommended reading

■ The Politics of Food

Not on the Label by Felicity Lawrence, Penguin 2004
Shopped by Joanna Blythman, HarperPerennial 2005
Fast Food Nation by Eric Schlosser, Penguin 2002

■ Raw classics

The Sunfood Diet Success System or anything else by David Wolfe
Rainbow Green Live Cuisine or anything else by Gabriel Cousens
Raw by Juliano, the original gourmet raw recipe book

■ Educational websites

www.thebestdayever.com David Wolfe's amazing website on raw foods and cutting edge nutrition.

www.newstarget.com Independent news on natural health, nutrition and more from Mike Adams and team.

www.whfoods.com The world's healthiest foods, comprehensive nutritional information from George Mateljan.

■ Index